# FAT TIRE

## TALES AND TRAILS

MUTANT approved!

"In the beginning, there was *FAT*!"
- *Genisis: The Fat Tire Bible*

photo: Tom Brownold

DRY LAKE HILLS, FLAGSTAFF

"Drink when you're thirsty. Whoop when you're high.
Love your sweet life. Ride 'till you die."

# - NEW MIGHTY MILLENNIUM -
# FAT TIRE TALES & TRAILS
## ARIZONA MOUNTAIN BIKE TRAIL GUIDE

### PUBLISHED BY COSMIC RAY
### FLAGSTAFF, ARIZONA

#### SPRING, 2001  (14TH EDITION)

Printed on recycled paper with blood, sweat and vegetable ink.

"We test our shred."

# RATING THE RIDES

For comparison's sake, all rides were rated by me, a seedy but sincere middle age male in reasonably good physical condition if otherwise unencumbered by the though process.

**EASY**: Some hills with nothing too steep or too long. A weenie ride. If you can't handle this you are one hopeless sofa-tater. I suggest more soda pop, Doritos and TV including shopping and game shows, golf, surgery, info-mercials, Survivor re-runs, soaps and channel surfing. Get plenty of quality couch time, high dollar gin, sex toys and video games. See a doctor.

**MODERATE:** Guaranteed to get the dead laughing and singing again. Interesting terrain with some healthy exposure to risk. Good sweaty, stinky, hard work, but still not killer.

**DIFFICULT:** Rough, tough, painful, hardass and muy dangeroso with occasional warp speed, climbing and distance. Not for the respiratorily challenged. Sort of like straight espresso. If you don't know what it is, you don't want it.

**EXTREME:** Caution! May set off low self esteem panic attack. Possible bloodbath. Parents would not approve. Nor your insurance agent, doctor, spouse or bike if it could talk. Also known as puck-10, no-brainer, e-ticket, hairball, burly, barny or barndog, abusive, gonzo, mongo, mondo, psycho, way super gnarly, hideous, hateful and gruesome. Do you lack common sense? Is your brain adrift in a sea of cheap beer or what.

"Saddle up effendi, we ride!"
-Aladdin

# TOOL KIT

## BE THOUGHT NEITHER CHURLISH LOUT, NOODGE NOR TRAIL TURD! KNOW HOW TO FIX A FLAT AND CARRY THY OWN KIT!

**SPARE PARTS:** Tube, patch kit, tire booting material, length of wire, chain link, spoke, duct tape and imagination.

**TOOLS:** combo tool (fix anything but a broken heart!)
chain tool (know how to use it)
tiny combo wrenches (8-9-10 mm)
petite hex (allen) wrenches (sizes to fit)
good mini-pump (check periodically)
tire irons (lose the screwdriver)
swiss army knife with corkscrew (you never know!)
sticks and stones (various sizes found on site)

**AND:** cell phone, small compass, T.P. and trowel (bury it deep!), fresh condom, matches, sunblock, a few crisp apples, one smoked salmon, a good hard cheese and a 1978 *SILVER OAK* Alexander Valley Cabernet to whittle away at the time.

# COSMIC WARNING!
## MOUNTAIN BIKING IS HAZARDOUS!

Despite what some slicker-than-a-cheap-chicken lawyer might whisper in your ear, it ain't my fault!

THEREFORE, Cosmic Ray must advise that mountain biking is risky as heck. I have scars to prove it! This book is no substitute for topo maps, route finding skill, compass, good judgement, sense of humor, manners or cognitive thought. Oh yeah, wear a helmet.

FURTHER, I've done my best. I'm not responsible for wind, weather, beasts, boners, big rocks, sign changes, puddles, detours or ANY misfortune that pegs the puck-o-meter or gets your butt fur in a knot.

MOREOVER upon buying or snaking this book and reading this disclaimer you release and discharge me, my heirs and representatives from mistakes, getting lost or wrecking. Hey, poop happens. Lighten up.

REALIZE that it ain't Ray's quackin' fault. It's YOUR responsibility to be familiar with route, road, trail, grief factor, weather, water supply, mechanical condition, mind set, companions, lions, tigers, bears, undies, acts of God, pump, patch kit, camel sack and every other dang thing.

FINALLY, it's OK to be weak of physique or lame of brain, but if you be thin of grin PLEASE STAY SAFE AT HOME! Thank You.

# AZ TRAIL TO WALNUT CYN.

**START**

TO LONE TREE RD. SEE "FISHER PT."

TO MARSHALL LAKE VIA AZ TRAIL SEE "FISHER POINT"

AZ TRAIL

CAVE

FISHER PT.

AZ TRAIL

ACCESS: SEE "FISHER POINT"

NOTE! ENDANGERED BIRD SPECIES NEST IN INNER WALNUT CANYON. NO BIKES PLEASE. EXPLORE ON FOOT ONLY.

**-LEGEND-**
—— PAVED ROAD
- - - DIRT ROAD
•••• SINGLE TRACK

**-SCALE-**
⊢1Mi.⊣

N

WALNUT CANYON

AZ TRAIL

TO CONTINENTAL COUNTRY CLUB 6 MILES

FS 303

TO OLD ROUTE 66 & I-40 EAST OF FLAGSTAFF EXIT 204 3 MILES

WALNUT CYN. NAT. MON. VISITOR CTR.

MONUMENT ROAD

# FLAGSTAFF

©97
RAY

# Flagstaff ARIZONA TRAIL
## SINGLE TRACK TO WALNUT CANYON

**DISTANCE:** 30 MILES R.T.
**TIME:** 5 HOURS
**EFFORT:** HARD RIDE
**SKILL:** ADVANCED
**PUCK-O-METER:** PUCK 4
  SOME TECHNICAL STUFF
**FIND ROUTE:** EASY
**SEASON:** APR to NOV

**AT A GLANCE**

9000

**ELEV. (FT.)**

6500

O   **LOOP MILES**   15

**DESCRIPTION:** Famous Flagstaff mountain biker Carl Tobin turned me on to this ride. He said he likes it because it has a bit of everything in great big doses. There is great single track carving, short tough climbs and descents as well as just enough technical stuff to keep you on your toes. And best of all, you ride 12 miles right on the rim of Walnut Canyon. On my first try I ran out of food by the time I got to the national monument visitor center and was not too proud to beg cookies from tourists alongside the local squirrels. Bring food!

**DIRECTIONS:** Find your way to Fisher Point. See the FISHER POINT map. You'll find yourself staring at a huge gorgeous sandstone cliff with a big cave hollowed out at the base. About 100 feet before the cave there is a trail to the left that takes you zig zagging steeply up to the top of the cliff and Fisher Point. Be sure to take the little detour on top to The Point and check out the view. Now get back on the main trail and continue all the way out to Walnut Canyon National Monument Visitor Center. Be sure to take every opportunity to run out to the rim for more views.

**OPTIONS:** Return the way you came or head home loop style via Monument Road (see map) and Old Route 66. A shorter easier option is to take FS 303 back to town. A lazy weenie possibility is to leave a car parked at the visitor center packed with Doritos, tunes and drinks. Yes!

*"24 hours in a day. 24 beers in a case. Coincidence?"*
*-ancient mystery*

# *Flagstaff* **DRY LAKE HILLS**
## GREAT SINGLE TRACK LOOP

**DISTANCE:** 9.3 MILES
**TIME:** 2 HOURS
**EFFORT:** HARD WORK
**SKILL:** EXPERT
**PUCK-O-METER:** PUCK 7
FAST DESCENT DOWN SCHULTZ CREEK
**FIND ROUTE:** EASY
**SEASON:** APR to NOV

**AT A GLANCE**

9000

**ELEV. (FT.)**

7000

O    **LOOP MILES**    9.3

**DESCRIPTION:** One of the best single track loops in the state. Starts at Schultz Creek parking area with a wicked tough 1-track up and over Rocky Ridge Trail to Elden Lookout Road. After a short jog up Lookout Road, tackle short but waaay steep Lower Brookbank Trail up to Dry Lake Hills. Take a deep breath or three at the top then head

**PRIMO** **TRAIL**

over to a ripping fast descent down Little Gnarly Trail to Schultz Creek Trail and back to START. This last bit down Schultz Creek is way fun with temptation to haul ass. Avoid stackage! Watch for upcoming riders and always yield to hikers. Also heads up for the occasional crazed motorcyclist on Schultz Creek Trail. These paths are all well marked with nice wooden signs.

**DIRECTIONS:** From downtown Flag head north out of town on HWY 180 toward The Grand Canyon. After only about 2 miles at milepost 218.6 you'll see the sign for Schultz Pass where you hang a right. Continue until the pavement ends, go through the gate and then take a short, steep right down into the parking area. Look around for that sign that says Rocky Ridge Trail.

**FLAGSTAFF**

# Flagstaff MOUNT ELDEN LOOP
## EPIC SINGLE TRACK LOOP

**DISTANCE:** 18.5 MILES
**TIME:** 3 TO 5 HOURS
**EFFORT:** BIBLICAL
**SKILL:** EXPERT
**PUCK-O-METER:** PUCK 6.5
   SOME FAST & TECHNICAL SECTIONS
**FIND ROUTE:** SIGNED
**SEASON:** APR to NOV

**AT A GLANCE**

9000

**ELEV.
(FT.)**

6500

O   **LOOP MILES**   18.5

**DESCRIPTION:** Mount Elden single track trails are legend. This loop connects the dots to circumnavigate the mountain. You'll call this siege epic . . . yup, epic, as in shoot the wounded, eat the weak! This be the real thing. The route is *mostly* signed. Keep Elden on your right. Follow the contour of the mountain. Take no false trail leading steep up nor down to town. Follow the signs. I've done this route a dozen times. The map is to scale and spot on.

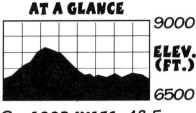

PRIMO TRAIL

## MILEAGE LOG

**0.0** START at Schultz Creek Trailhead and head up Schultz Creek Trail. See the map.

**3.0** Gate. CONTINUE straight and up.

**3.6** Sunset Trail Trailhead. Hop on Sunset.

**4.0** LEFT onto Little Elden Trail around Schultz Tank and head down killer single track.

**5.7** Little Bear flashes by on your right. IGNORE.

**8.6** HEADS UP! After Sandy Seep, easy to miss turn coming up. See map. Take a RIGHT. More great single track to Fatman's Loop.

**11.1** Across the bottom of Fatman's then the trail takes a tricky jog. Hop on Pipeline Trail. Signed.

**14.2** Lower Oldham Trail. Take a RIGHT up and steep over to Elden Lookout Road.

**15.5** Legs like jello? Get ready for Rocky Ridge! Rough tough and technical.

**18.5** Back to go. May I suggest a cold one or two.

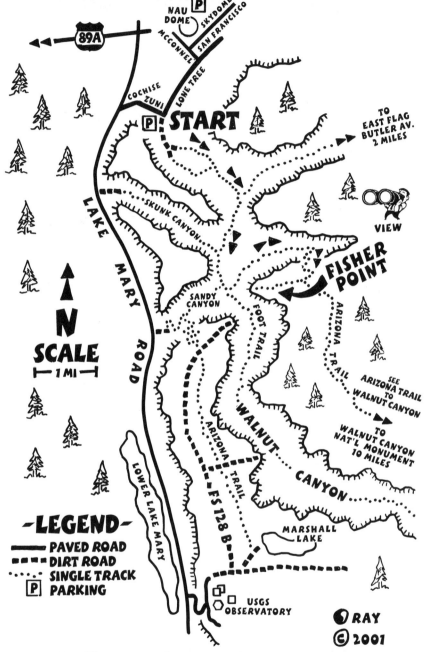

# FLAGSTAFF

FISHER POINT

# Flagstaff **FISHER POINT**
## EASY SINGLE TRACK TO LOVELY SPOT

**DISTANCE:** 7.2 MILES
**TIME:** 2 to 2.5 HOURS
**EFFORT:** COMFORTABLE
**SKILL:** ROOKIE
**PUCK-O-METER:** PUCK 2
NO FEAR WHATSOEVER
**FIND ROUTE:** SIMPLE
**SEASON:** APR to NOV

**AT A GLANCE**

8000

**ELEV.
(FT.)**

6500

O **1-WAY MILES** 3.6

**DESCRIPTION:** This easy single track is perfect for the novice rider. I took my 2-year-old daughter in her baby seat. Secluded Fisher Point is primo for a picnic, sunbath or grooving on the humongo Coconino sandstone rock face and its cave at the entrance to Walnut Canyon. Park your bike here and explore the canyon floor on foot. Walnut Canyon is cool and quiet with lots of birds and a great cave a half mile or so on your right.

**DIRECTIONS:** Have a look at the map and find the N.A.U. Skydome. Start where paved Lone Tree makes a sharp right and becomes Zuni. Straight onto the dirt road and continue until the trail splits after the first mile. Go either way as they rejoin a mile later. After another mile the trail splits again. Avoid a bummer ride to East Flag and Butler Av. unless you like barking dogs, motels and traffic. Instead, go right to a splendid day at Fisher Point. Return the way you came.

**OPTIONS:** Check out the map. If you feel energetic you can do the longer 25 mile round trip ride out to Marshal Lake on the well marked AZ Trail and return via Lake Mary Road. You have a short steep climb out of Sandy Canyon, but the rest is easy and smooth all the way.

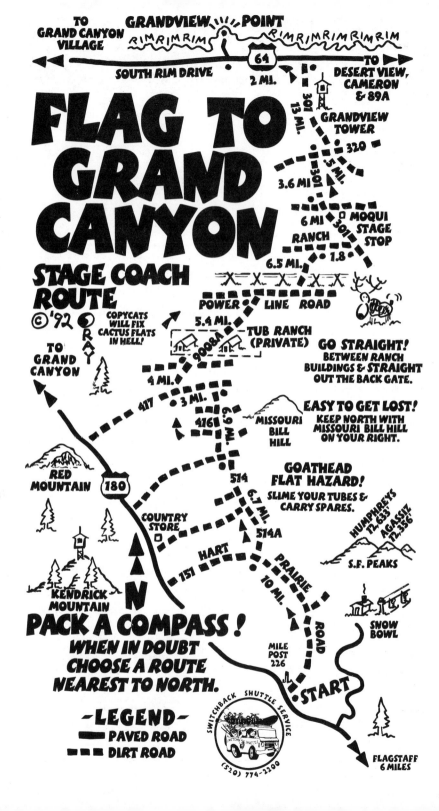

# Flagstaff **TO GRAND CANYON**
## HISTORIC STAGE COACH ROUTE

**DISTANCE:** 70 MILES
**TIME:** 2 DAYS
**EFFORT:** LONG EASY RIDE
**SKILL:** EASY DIRT ROADS
**PUCK-O-METER:** PUCK 2
DON'T GET LOST. BRING A COMPASS
**FIND ROUTE:** EASY
**SEASON:** APR to NOV

**AT A GLANCE**

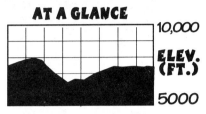

10,000

**ELEV. (FT.)**

5000

O **1-WAY MILES** 70

**DESCRIPTION:** Moqui Station was one of three stops enroute Flag to The Canyon, 1892 to 1899. A 12 hour trip cost $20 (1890s dollars!) and ran three times a week with six-horse coaches and a trailer. On September 7, 1897 Coconino Cycling Club team captain C. H. Coble and his studly crew beat the stage to The South Rim on their trusty 1-speeds!

An 1890s writer said, "The road is good and level with some heavy grades. It winds among the slopes of the San Francisco Mountains for the first 25 miles through a fine forest of pine. The next 25 miles lead across a rolling prairie and the rest through the forest which skirts the rim of The Grand Canyon. Riders will find advantage to fit wheels with a gear not exceeding 66 inches. To The Grand Canyon is 70 miles. Any rider can do it in 8 to 12 hours." On 1-speed clunkers yet!

This is an ideal 2-day tour. The gate where FS 417 meets 9008A is a good spot to meet your support. Bring lots of water, food and tubes for goathead thorns. SLIME tube sealant recommended!

COCONINO CYCLING CLUB AT THE GRAND CANYON, SEPTEMBER 7, 1897

FLAGSTAFF

# LAVA CAVE & WING MTN.

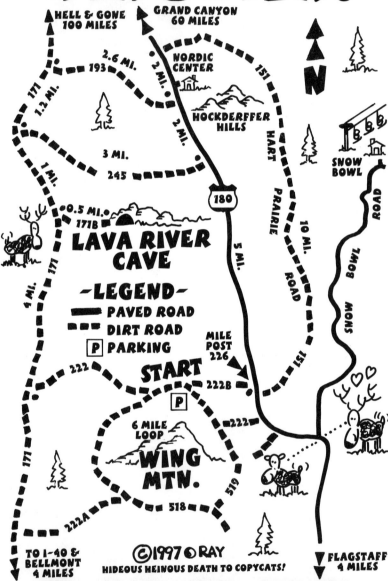

HELL & GONE
100 MILES

GRAND CANYON
60 MILES

N

2.6 MI.
193

177

1.2 MI.

NORDIC
CENTER

151

HOCKDERFFER
HILLS

SNOW
BOWL

2 MI.

2 MI.

SNOW BOWL ROAD

3 MI.

245

1 MI.

180

5 MI.

HART PRAIRIE ROAD

10 MI.

0.5 MI.
171B

171

LAVA RIVER
CAVE

-LEGEND-

━━━ PAVED ROAD

╍╍╍ DIRT ROAD

P PARKING

4 MI.

177

222

MILE
POST
226

START

222B

151

P

6 MILE
LOOP

WING
MTN.

222

171

222A

518

519

TO I-40 &
BELLMONT
4 MILES

© 1997 © RAY
HIDEOUS HEINOUS DEATH TO COPYCATS!

FLAGSTAFF
4 MILES

# FLAGSTAFF

# Flagstaff **LAVA RIVER CAVE**
## EASY FOREST ROADS TO COOL CAVE

**DISTANCE:** 30 MILE LOOP
**TIME:** 5 HOURS
**EFFORT:** MODERATE
**SKILL:** EASY
**PUCK-O-METER:** PUCK ?
AFRAID OF THE DARK?
**FIND ROUTE:** EASY
**SEASON:** APR to NOV

**AT A GLANCE**

10,000

**ELEV.
(FT.)**

5000

O   **LOOP MILES**   30

**DESCRIPTION:** Extending nearly a mile under the forest, Lava River Cave gets tight in one spot, but the ceiling is 30 feet high in another. Bring a snack, plenty of water, 3 flashlights and warm clothing. The cave is quite cool and dark and this is no place for a panic attack! Discovered by loggers in 1915, this is the longest lava tube in Arizona. Formed 700,000 years ago, lava ran from a nearby volcano then cooled on the top and bottom while continuing to flow and then emptied creating a tube.

The long smooth dirt road out to Lava Cave sports views of The Peaks through a fine open forest of pine and aspen along a gentle climb. No food or water en route.

**DIRECTIONS:** Start at the parking area near Wing Mountain and follow the map to the cave. Return via HWY 180 or Hart Prairie Road for a nice long easy loop.

**OPTION:** The smooth and easy 6-mile Aspen Loop around Wing Mountain makes for an ideal family trek, especially in the fall when the aspen leaves are blazing.

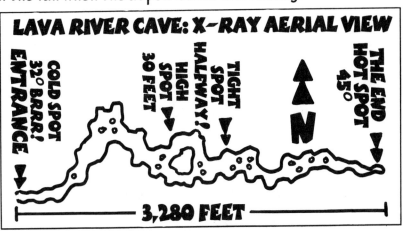

LAVA RIVER CAVE: X-RAY AERIAL VIEW

COLD SPOT 32° BRRR! ENTRANCE

HIGH SPOT 30 FEET

HALFWAY!

TIGHT SPOT

N

THE END HOT SPOT 45°

3,280 FEET

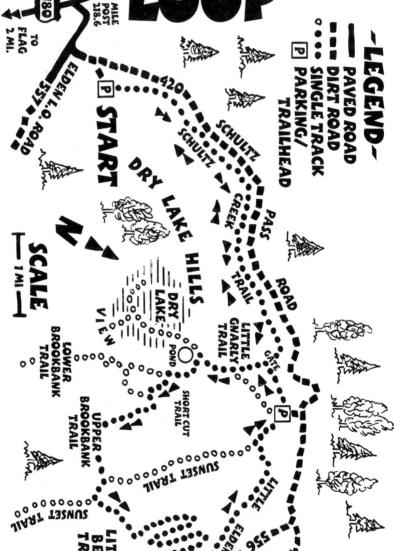

# LITTLE BEAR LOOP

**FLAGSTAFF**

© RAY
©1999

# Flagstaff **LITTLE BEAR LOOP**
## RAY'S FAVORITE SINGLE TRACK LOOP

**DISTANCE:** 17.3 MILES
**TIME:** 3 to 4 HOURS
**EFFORT:** SERIOUS CLIMB
**SKILL:** ADVANCED
**PUCK-O-METER:** PUCK 8
TWO FAST SINGLE TRACK DESCENTS
**FIND ROUTE:** FAIR EASY
**SEASON:** APR to NOV

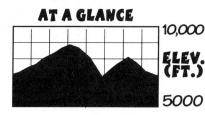

**AT A GLANCE**

10,000

**ELEV. (FT.)**

5000

O    **LOOP MILES**    17.3

PRIMO

TRAIL

**DESCRIPTION:** Yell "YES!" so loud that local squirrels think somebody musta got lucky. Single track climbs, descents, switchbacks and views high along Flag's best trails link up to make this ride epic. Crank up Schultz Creek Trail, grind up Little Gnarly and up Upper Brookbank, fly down Little Bear, up Little Elden and finally, blast down twisty-turny Schultz Creek to the finish. Just say YES!

### MILEAGE LOG

0.0 START at Schultz Creek trailhead (see map) and enjoy a very fine, all do-able climb up Schultz Creek.

3.6 Gate. Go RIGHT up Little Gnarly. Stay right and climb all the way up to a little pond.

4.7 Lovely small pond. Go LEFT on single track.

4.8 LEFT up for a short, steep single track short cut.

4.9 LEFT onto Upper Brookbank. More tough climbing.

6.9 AHHH! The top. Now bear right down Sunset Trail.

7.2 LEFT at top of Little Bear. Down and fast. Be ready for hikers and horses. Mind your manners.

10.9 LEFT onto Little Elden and a short climb back up.

12.8 RIGHT onto Sunset Trail.

13.1 Sunset Trailhead parking lot. Go across the lot and head down Schultz Creek Trail.

13.7 Gate. You were here on the way up. Go back through gate and enjoy wicked fun descent. You earned this twisting, turning, jumping descent.

17.3 Finish. Whaddaya think? Best ride ever? Heck YES!

*"I thought of that while riding my bike." - Albert Einstein*

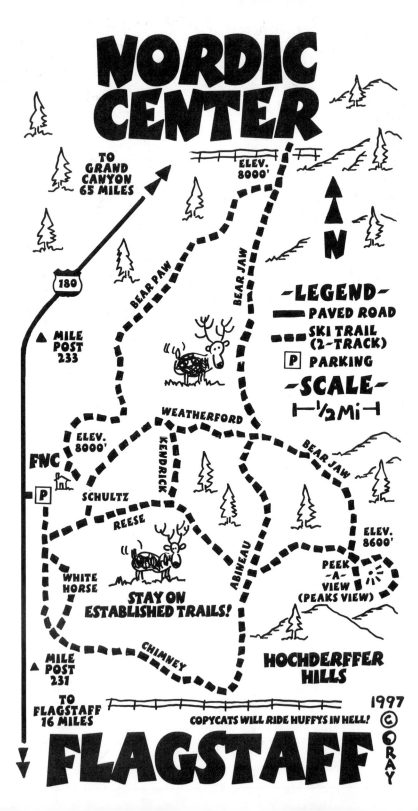

# Flagstaff *NORDIC SKI CENTER*
## EASY 2-TRACK SKI TO SCENIC SPOT

**DISTANCE:** 2 to 25 MILES
**TIME:** 0.5 to 3 HOURS
**EFFORT:** EASY to MEDIUM
**SKILL:** NOVICE
**PUCK-O-METER:** PUCK 2
NO FEAR ON EASY DESCENTS
**FIND ROUTE:** MODERATE
**SEASON:** MAY to NOV

**AT A GLANCE**

9500

**ELEV. (FT.)**

7000

O **LOOP MILES** 25

**DESCRIPTION:** High in the snowy aspen above town the manicured XC ski trails of the Flagstaff Nordic Center are deep in snow all winter. A snow cat sets a double ski track to guide your way through the crispy cold air. A skating lane is set for aerobic animals like me . . . in my dreams! When spring rolls around they park the Pisten Bully and hang up the skinny skis. The National Forest trails dry and it's time to rock and roll.

Open 8 days a week all summer, the trails are free fat tire fun. Huge aspen groves punctuate the towering ponderosa pine forest. The technicolor leaf display peaks around October 1. I've jumped an early morning fall herd of 50 elk. The views extend to a picture perfect up close telephoto shot of The Peaks and Snowbowl from Peak-a-View. Families and new riders love the easy to moderate double-track trails with no steep climbs. Not much danger of getting lost either. The summer trails are unmarked, but the whole place is surrounded by a fence. Just head downhill and you're back to your car.

More serious hammerheads who feel that need for speed find the trails interesting and uncrowded. When it's 113$^{\circ}$ in Phoenix, it's in the early to mid-seventies up here. Wear your helmet, carry food, water and emergency rain gear. The summer monsoon is wicked wet, but over quick.

"A life without bikes ain't no life at all."
- Sonny Barger, Hell's Angels

**FLAGSTAFF**

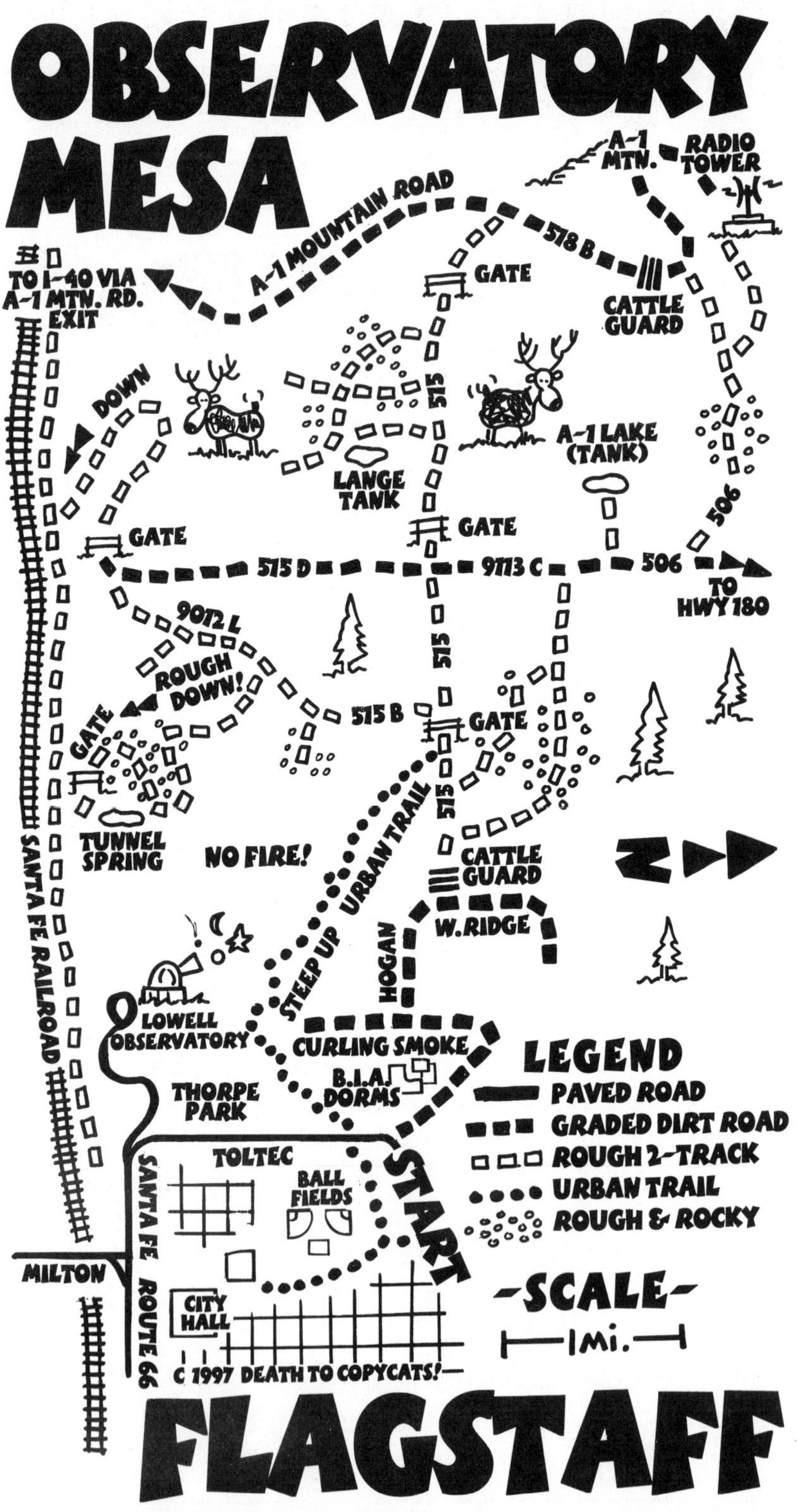

# OBSERVATORY MESA

A-1 MTN. RADIO TOWER

A-1 MOUNTAIN ROAD

518 B

GATE

CATTLE GUARD

TO I-40 VIA A-1 MTN. RD. EXIT

DOWN

515

A-1 LAKE (TANK)

506

LANGE TANK

GATE

GATE

515 D

9113 C

506

TO HWY 180

9012 L

515

ROUGH DOWN!

515 B

GATE

GATE

515

TUNNEL SPRING

NO FIRE!

STEEP UP

URBAN TRAIL

HOGAN

CATTLE GUARD

W. RIDGE

LOWELL OBSERVATORY

CURLING SMOKE

B.I.A. DORMS

SANTA FE RAILROAD

THORPE PARK

TOLTEC

BALL FIELDS

START

## LEGEND

——— PAVED ROAD

■■■ GRADED DIRT ROAD

▢▢▢ ROUGH 2-TRACK

••• URBAN TRAIL

ROUGH & ROCKY

MILTON

SANTA FE ROUTE 66

CITY HALL

C 1997 DEATH TO COPYCATS!

-SCALE-
⊢—1 mi.—⊣

# FLAGSTAFF

# Flagstaff OBSERVATORY MESA
## CLOSE-TO-TOWN FOREST TRAILS

**DISTANCE:** 2 to 20 MILES
**TIME:** 1 TO 3 HOURS
**EFFORT:** WEENIE RIDE
**SKILL:** NOVICE
**PUCK-O-METER:** PUCK 4
CAUTION ON URBAN TRAIL DESCENT
**FIND ROUTE:** MODERATE
**SEASON:** APR to NOV

**AT A GLANCE**

8500

**ELEV. (FT.)**

6000

0     **MILES**     20

**DESCRIPTION:** So many roads that even the elk get lost! Percival Lowell got lost and built his observatory 100 years ago with the family fortune to look for Pluto and life on Mars. Bet his parents loved that. No life found on Mars . . . so far.

Golden barked old Ponderosa pine giants shade the forest below. Massive elk with majestic racks migrate here in fall. I got wet and nearly froze my toes one very late fall. Ow!

Access is via a steep 500 ft. climb onto the mesa up an Urban Trail (see map). Orientation is easy. The San Francisco Peaks are in sight northeast. The main road is FS 515. Close all gates and respect private property. Loops are possible under the forest canopy then down Tunnel Springs and follow the RR tracks to town. A rocky hellacious descent to Tunnel Springs is quite the hairball buttruff (i.e. Too easy to ride standing up, but too rough to ride comfortably seated!). E-ticket fun, but crazy not to wear a helmet.

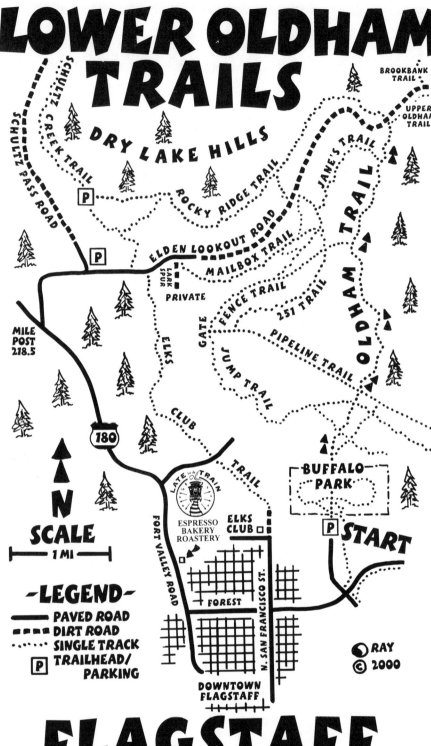

# Flagstaff LOWER OLDHAM TRAIL
## BIG FUN SINGLE TRACK PLAY AREA

**DISTANCE:** 3.6 MILES
**TIME:** 1 HOUR PLUS ???
**EFFORT:** NO SWEAT
**SKILL:** DARN EASY
**PUCK-O-METER:** PUCK 4
SOME BOULDERS TO GET THROUGH
**FIND ROUTE:** MODERATE
**SEASON:** APR to NOV

**AT A GLANCE**

8500

**ELEV. (FT.)**

6000

O **1-WAY MILES** 3.6

**FLAGSTAFF**

**DESCRIPTION:** Lower Oldham Trail cuts through a maze of some of the coolest single track around. If you love to carve some fairly level groove with only an occasional short technical bit, this is for you.

Lower Oldham is a favorite route connecting Buffalo Park with Mt. Elden Trail System. Connections exist to Upper Oldham, Rocky Ridge, Schultz Creek, Sunset, Pipeline and Brookbank Trails, but first I suggest thorough exploration of the 1-track playground weaving in and around Lower Oldham. It's close to town, gently rolling and just challenging enough to get your butt fur dialed for the rest of the day.

Although my map is pretty complete, there is a welter of trail here. The whole area only covers only about 4 square miles and is surrounded on all sides by roads or steep boulder walls. You can't get too lost. Stay out of anything that looks like private property and watch for hikers, especially on weekends.

**DIRECTIONS:** Easy as pie to find. Begin from either end at Buffalo Park or Elden Lookout Road. Buffalo Park has good parking and also provides a safe and car-less access. Don't ride on danger HWY 180. My map also shows the secret local's access via private property at your own risk, but you didn't hear it from me.

*"I'm not afraid of dying, I just don't want to be there when it happens."*
*-Woody Allen*

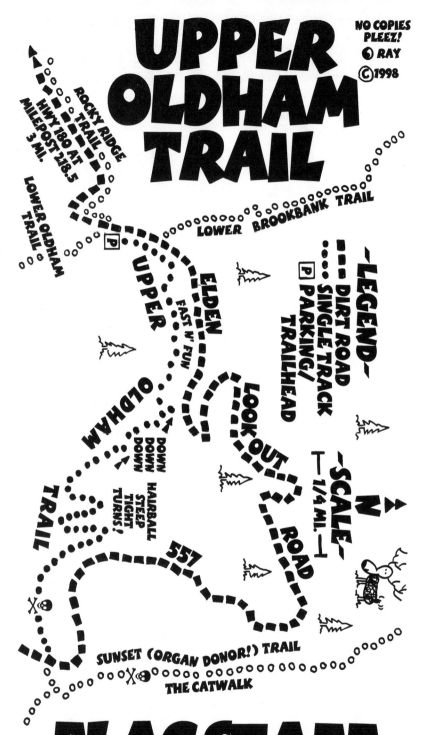

# Flagstaff UPPER OLDHAM TRAIL
## KILLER STEEP 1-TRACK DESCENT

**DISTANCE:** 4.4 MILE LOOP
**TIME:** 1 to 1.5 HOURS
**EFFORT:** HEINOUS CLIMB
**SKILL:** EXPERT
**PUCK-O-METER:** PUCK 9
STEEP, TWISTING, TECHNICAL DESCENT
**FIND ROUTE:** SIMPLE
**SEASON:** APR to NOV

**AT A GLANCE**

9000

**ELEV. (FT.)**

7500

O **1-WAY MILES** 2.2

**DESCRIPTION:** OK, OK, so it's not the longest trail in the world, but not the most boring either . . . and it hooks up with some other mighty shreddage. It's one of my secret faves, so you might like it too. Next time you find yourself at the top of Mt. Elden, give it a go. It's signed at the top. Use caution or you could get spanked.

Now the bad news . . . first you gotta get to the top of Elden. Boo-hoo. If you *drive* up, SHAME! You should be home in front of your TV taking your little titty-baby nap. The granny gear grind up Elden Road is soul food.

**OPTIONS:** Try the ride up Schultz Creek, up Little Gnarly, over Dry Lake and down Lower Brookbank, *then* 2.2 miles up Elden Road to the top of Upper Oldham and down to Rocky Ridge. Makes for one kick ass 11 mile loop!

Lower Upper Oldham (a.k.a. Middle Oldham or Newham Trail) meets Lower Oldham trail system at the bottom (see the Lower Oldham Trail map on the previous pages), so there is still a heap of great single track descending to be had. I usually wind up at Macy's Coffee House chugging a double cap, eating some gooey treat and licking my wounds. Yuck!

**DIRECTIONS:** Head north 2 miles out of Flag on HWY 180 to milepost 218.5. The sign says Schultz Pass Road. Hang a right and go about a mile to where the road splits. Elden Lookout is the right fork. It's paved and flat at first but later gets steep and goes all to hell.

"In the end, all solutions are temporary."
American Duct Tape Council

# Flagstaff **AROUND THE PEAKS**
## ARIZONA'S COSMIC PEAK EXPERIENCE

**DISTANCE:** 46 MILES
**TIME:** ALL DAY
**EFFORT:** FAIRLY TOUGH
**SKILL:** NOT AT ALL TRICKY
**PUCK-O-METER:** PUCK 6.5
SOME VERY SPEEDY DESCENTS
**FIND ROUTE:** MODERATE
**SEASON:** APR to NOV

**AT A GLANCE**

10,000

**ELEV. (FT.)**

5000

O   **LOOP MILES**   45

**DESCRIPTION:** An epic jeep road loop circles The San Francisco Peaks thru a picturesque forest of pine and aspen. Follow Cosmic Soulstice race loop for a tough 1-day ride or you may prefer a leisurely 2-day tour meeting support at Lockett Meadow for a splendid campout under the stars. Knee popping climbs. Hair raising descents. Long rolls thru open forest and vast views. Respiratorily challenged whiners need not apply! If you're into *zen and the up* or you like to get higher than a hippie in a helicopter during fall colors, hop on!

**DIRECTIONS:** Follow map to Schultz Tank START.  Head up Weatherford Trail across the road from parking lot. Go 1.6 miles to Aspen Spring then LEFT 4.2 miles down to Snow Bowl Road. Now go up to milepost 5.5 and LEFT through the fence down to Hart Prairie Rd. Follow Hart Prairie 5.5 miles to FS 418. Right on 418 for 11 miles to Lost Tank. Go RIGHT 1 mile to Lockett Meadow Rd., RIGHT up to Lockett Meadow, take the first RIGHT just after a small shed up to the cabins then a 7 mile screaming descent back to START. Whew!

# ROCKY RIDGE TRAIL

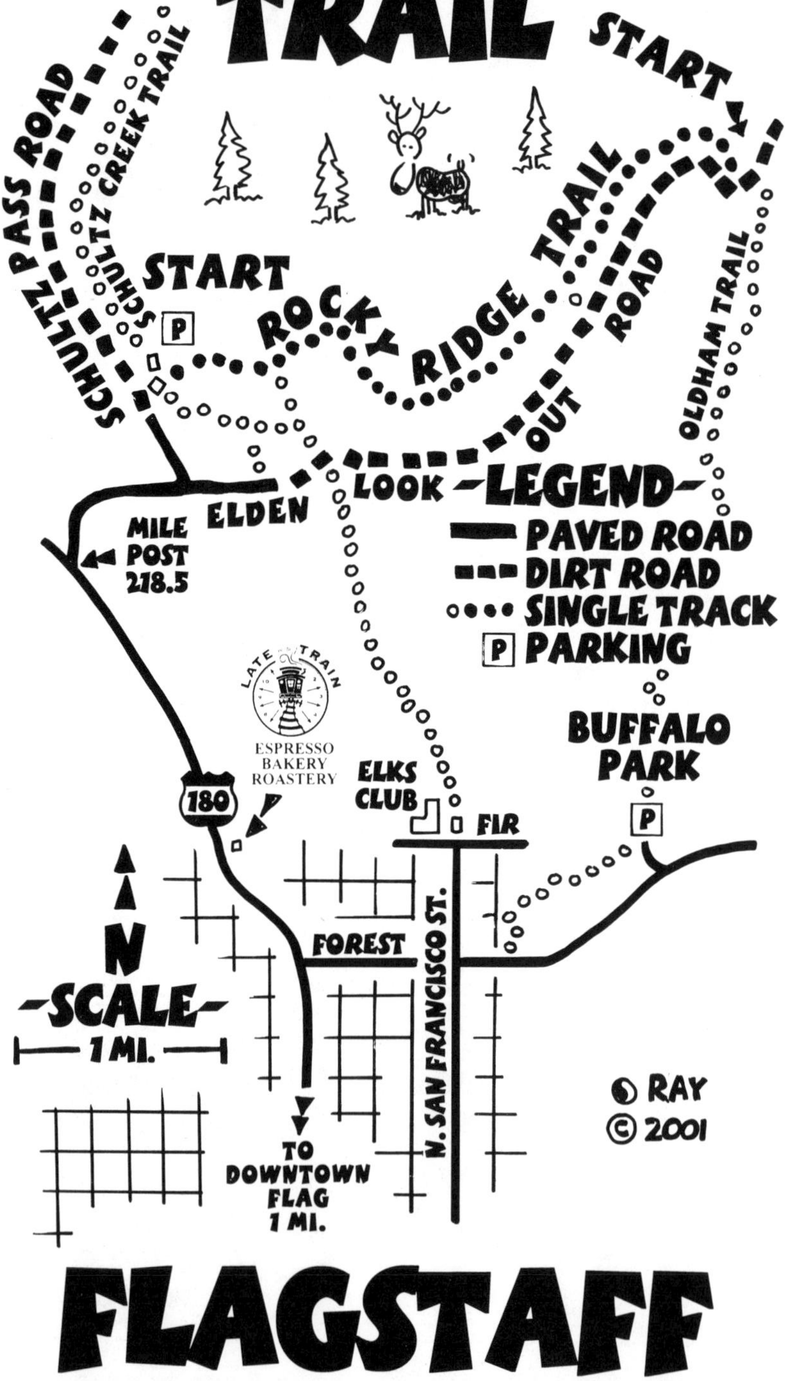

START

SCHULTZ PASS ROAD

SCHULTZ CREEK TRAIL

START

ROCKY RIDGE TRAIL

OUT ROAD

OLDHAM TRAIL

ELDEN LOOK

MILE POST 218.5

LATE TRAIN
ESPRESSO BAKERY ROASTERY

180

ELKS CLUB

FIR

BUFFALO PARK

FOREST

N. SAN FRANCISCO ST.

N

SCALE
1 MI.

TO DOWNTOWN FLAG 1 MI.

## ~LEGEND~
PAVED ROAD
DIRT ROAD
SINGLE TRACK
P PARKING

© RAY
© 2001

# FLAGSTAFF

**DISTANCE:** 3.0 MILES
**TIME:** 0.5 to 1 HOUR
**EFFORT:** HARD FUN WORK
**SKILL:** EXPERTO
**PUCK-O-METER:** PUCK 8
SO EASY TO WRECK ON THE ROCKS.
**FIND ROUTE:** EASY
**SEASON:** MAR to NOV

AT A GLANCE

8500

ELEV.
(FT.)

6000

0   **1 WAY MILES**   3.0

**DESCRIPTION:** Gravity school is in session. Maintain thy rolling speed lest the earth rise up and smite thee. Close-to-town, rolling, technical single track through a forest of ponderosa pine, Gambel oak and old twisty, gnarled alligator bark juniper. Favored by local mountain bikers because of challenging terrain, convenient location and fun shortcut connection between Mount Elden Lookout Road trails and Schultz Pass Road trails. Sets of baby head to television size boulders interrupt otherwise smooth, rolling topography. The top half from Elden Road down, drops about 200 feet making for great momentum. Then the technical shreddage starts as the trail rolls up and down across Rocky Ridge.

**DIRECTIONS:** North out of Flag on HWY 180 for 2 miles to milepost 218.6. Turn right at Schultz Pass sign and follow the map up Elden Lookout Road. A sign on the left says Rocky Ridge. May the force be with you.

FLAGSTAFF

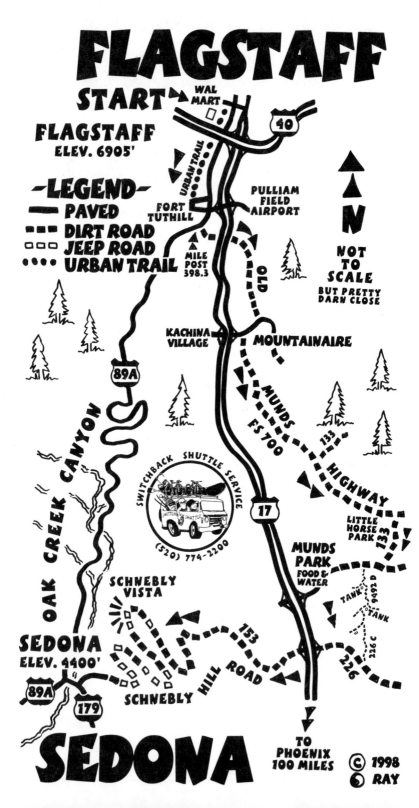

# Flagstaff FLAG TO SEDONA
## VIA OLD MUNDS HIWAY & SCHNEBLY HILL

**DISTANCE:** 43.8 MILES
**TIME:** ALL DAY
**EFFORT:** LOOOOONG RIDE
**SKILL:** MOSTLY EASY
**PUCK-O-METER:** PUCK 4
(You'll be tired on the long descent.)
**ROUTE:** ONE TRICKY SPOT
**SEASON:** MAY to NOV

**AT A GLANCE**

8,000

ELEV. (FT.)

3000

0   1-WAY MILES  43.8

**DESCRIPTION:** Old logging and wagon roads from Flagstaff pines to Sedona red rocks. Pass through stands of ponderosa pines and aspen before dropping into juniper and pinyon. Drop 3000 ft. in 6 miles. Pause to scope out one of the best views on the planet. Breakfast in Mountainaire, lunch in Munds Park and party in Sedona. Have a shuttle waiting in Sedona!

### MILEAGE LOG

**0.0** START south on urban trail next to Wal-Mart, across from Red Lobster, corner of McConnell and Beulah.

**3.0** Fort Tuthill County Fairgrounds. Head out to HWY 89A.

**3.5** RIGHT turn on paved 89A. Watch for cars.

**4.2** LEFT onto dirt road Old Munds Highway at milepost 398.3 directly across from *Jackson's Grill*.

**7.3** Jog RIGHT on paved Mountainaire Road.

**7.6** LEFT onto FS 700, Old Munds Highway. It's a long roll past Newman Park & Coyote Park to Little Horse Park.

**20.6** RIGHT turn on FS 133 at sign "Little Horse Park".

**22.4** RIGHT again on FS 240. Next comes the easy-to-miss turn in EXACTLY 1.25 miles.

**23.7** Old 2-track on left is FS9492D. Tricky route finding here. Find your way by keeping south (LEFT at 1st tank, RIGHT at 2nd tank, LEFT at "Y") OR you can cheat into Munds Park, have a snack and short cut on I-17 to Schnebly Hill Rd.

**28.8** "T" into FS 226. Go RIGHT onto Schnebly Hill Road and down Schnebly all the way to Sedona.

**43.8** SEDONA! Tired? Hungry? You are somewhat dazed and confused, but you are also one AWESOME POSSUM!

"To be old and wise, you must first be young and stupid."
-Cosmic Ray's College of Knowledge

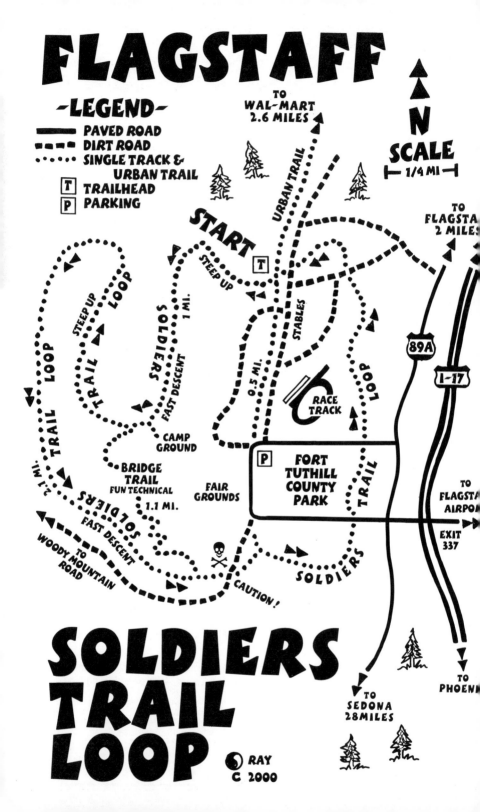

# Flagstaff SOLDIERS TRAIL
## QUICK LOOP AT TUTHILL

**DISTANCE:** 5 MILES PLUS
**TIME:** 1 HOUR PLUS
**EFFORT:** GO FAST
BREATHE HARD
**SKILL:** EASY
**PUCK-O-METER:** PUCK 3
ONE FAST DESCENT WITH GOOD TURNS
**FIND ROUTE:** SIGNED
**SEASON:** ALL YEAR

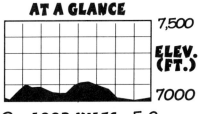

AT A GLANCE

7,500

ELEV.
(FT.)

7000

O    **LOOP MILES**    5.0

**DESCRIPTION:** Close to town. Easy to moderate. Some wide trail. Some interesting single track. East and south facing makes for long snow free season and good for cross country skis when it does snow. Even open when all other areas close down due to fire danger.

The 5 mile loop has two good climbs and some fun fast descents. The tread is not too challenging so it's great for beginners. It's all marked. There is also a way bitchin new technical section called Bridge Trail that bisects the main loop. It's only 1.1 miles each way, but the added 2.2 miles can really make the whole thing a hammer fest, especially if you ride out from town via the Ft. Tuthill Urban Trail from Wal-Mart. Hats off to the crew that built Bridge Trail with us mountain bikers in mind. They left in some good roots, rocks, dips, drops and even hand built a narrow little stone bridge.

To do the whole enchilada from town adds up to about 12 miles. At speed it may take some under an hour, but I'd allow 1.5 to 2.5 hours for most folks. I prefer the loop counter-clockwise because the climbs are steep and short and the descents are loooong, twisty and fast.

**DIRECTIONS:** Find the Flagstaff Wal-Mart. Good place to park, buy corn dogs and look at strange people. Urp! Urban trail starts along the east side of the parking lot next to the Wal-Mart garden center. It is well marked with a big sign. Head south until you get to a big trailhead sign by the dressage/horse jump area at Ft. Tuthill.

"The greatest risk is never taking one."
- Jackie Robinson

# *Flagstaff* **SUNSET TRAIL**
## *THE EPIC SINGLE TRACK LOOP*

**DISTANCE:** 14.6 MILES
**TIME:** 2.5 to 3.5 HOURS
**EFFORT:** ONE LONG CLIMB
**SKILL:** EXPERTO
**PUCK-O-METER:** PUCK 8.5
"ORGAN DONOR" TRAIL IS FOR REAL.
**ROUTE FINDING:** EASY
**SEASON:** APR to NOV

**AT A GLANCE**

10,000

**ELEV. (FT.)**

5000

O   **LOOP MILES**   14.6

**DESCRIPTION:** Jammin' down Sunset at mach speed will make your pants dance! A narrow, widowmaker catwalk, an 8-mile single track descent through a big boulder hobbit fern forest and ultra mondo killer twisty-turny finish make this loop epic. Whether you ride the full metal Huffy (good luck!) or a high dollar Ti Dream Weenie, this ride is sweeter than music that paints pictures. If you drove to the top so you can skank merrily DOWN the hill, SHAME! You are a lame ass corndog. *No guts, no glory!*

PRIMO TRAIL

### **MILEAGE LOG**

**0.0** Head up Elden Lookout Road. Figure 1 hour for the climb. (Record is 26 minutes!) Crank up the miles.

**7.0** Whew and yahoo! You did it! Sign directs you up a steep trail on LEFT 50 ft. to Sunset Trail. LEFT on Sunset. The skinny catwalk, Organ Donor Trail (no joke) is etched on the cliff. EXTREME CAUTION!

**8.8** Trail splits. Bear LEFT onto Upper Brookbank Trail. Go up a little then a way fun single track descent.

**10.5** EASY TO MISS! You are enjoying a fast, rough, rocky root infested descent when an unmarked trail heads sharply uphill to your RIGHT to Dry Lake.

**10.6** CONTINUE as you skirt the Dry Lake and head down ultra fun Little Gnarly Trail to Schultz Creek Trail.

**10.8** A loop Trail Junction. Bear LEFT and CONTINUE.

**11.6** Schultz Creek Trail. Go LEFT and enjoy one of the best single track descents in the western world.

**14.6** YES! Back to GO.

# FLAGSTAFF FALL COLORS

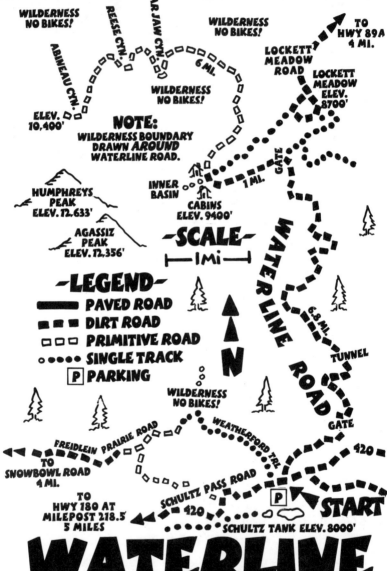

WILDERNESS NO BIKES!

REESE CYN.

BEAR JAW CYN.

ABINEAU CYN.

6 MI.

WILDERNESS NO BIKES!

WILDERNESS NO BIKES!

TO HWY 89A 4 MI.

LOCKETT MEADOW ROAD

LOCKETT MEADOW ELEV. 8700'

ELEV. 10,400'

**NOTE:**
WILDERNESS BOUNDARY DRAWN *AROUND* WATERLINE ROAD.

HUMPHREYS PEAK ELEV. 12,633'

AGASSIZ PEAK ELEV. 12,356'

INNER BASIN

CABINS ELEV. 9400'

1 MI.

GATE

WATERLINE ROAD

**SCALE**
├── 1 MI ──┤

**LEGEND**
▬▬▬ **PAVED ROAD**
■ ■ ■ **DIRT ROAD**
▢▢▢ **PRIMITIVE ROAD**
∘•••• **SINGLE TRACK**
🄿 **PARKING**

6.8 MI.

TUNNEL

N

WILDERNESS NO BIKES!

WEATHERFORD TRL.

GATE

FREIDLEIN PRAIRIE ROAD

TO SNOWBOWL ROAD 4 MI.

SCHULTZ PASS ROAD

420

420

🄿

START

TO HWY 180 AT MILEPOST 218.5 5 MILES

420

SCHULTZ TANK ELEV. 8000'

# WATERLINE ROAD

©1997 RAY

# Flagstaff **WATERLINE ROAD**
## FALL COLORS ON THE PEAKS

**DISTANCE:** 25 MILES
**TIME:** ALL DAY
**EFFORT:** LONG CLIMB
**SKILL:** SPEED CONTROL
**PUCK-O-METER:** PUCK 7.5
VERY HIGH SPEED DESCENT
**FIND ROUTE:** NO PROB
**SEASON:** MAY to OCT

**AT A GLANCE**

11,000

**ELEV. (FT.)**

6000

O **1-WAY MILES** 12.5

**DESCRIPTION:** Summer aspen leaves shimmer silver and green. A blast of stained glass color tints the aspen around October 1 before skeletal winter bares its snowy bleached bark bones. The essential Flagstaff Fall Leaf Looker is a 25 total mile *turn-and-burn* (out-and-back) all the way up Waterline Road to where it ends at Abineau Canyon. For the weenie riders there is also a short cut easier route.

**DIRECTIONS:** Caught your attention with mention of an easy route, eh? OK, head north out of Flag on HWY 89A to Lockett Meadow Road at milepost 431.2. Drive the 4.5 miles up to Lockett Meadow and park. Now hop on your bike and ride or walk a rough and tough 1 mile up to "the cabins". See the map. Turn RIGHT at the cabins and roll out to Abineau under a canopy of red and gold. This will be a total of 14 miles out and back with little climbing except for that first mile. I've seen this road 6 inches deep in a carpet of gold. If you get a wild hair, send the car home with a sofa spud and ride 20 miles all the way downhill via Schultz Pass Road to Flag. It's a gas, but WEAR A HELMET!

And for you *REAL* riders . . . head out of Flag on HWY 180 to milepost 218.5. Turn RIGHT and follow Schultz Pass Road 5 miles all the way up to Schultz Pass and the parking area at Schultz Tank. Out of the lot turn RIGHT and then a quick LEFT on Waterline Road FS 146. Ride all the way up to "the cabins" and continue another 6 miles beyond to the end at Abineau Canyon. You will be rewarded with hard work, sweat, a warm feeling in the seat of your pants . . . and the ability to look down your nose at all those who took the weenie option. You earned that cold frosty brew pop you left in the cooler!

> "Always do sober what you said you'd do while drunk.
> That will teach you to keep your mouth shut."
> - Ernest Hemmingway

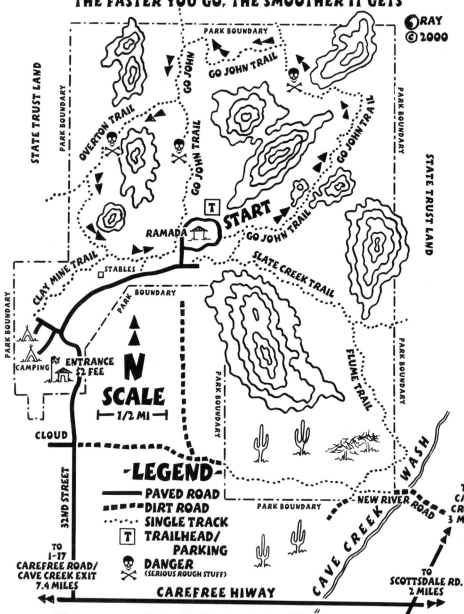

# CAVE CREEK

## "THE FASTER YOU GO, THE SMOOTHER IT GETS"

RAY © 2000

PARK BOUNDARY

GO JOHN TRAIL

GO JOHN

STATE TRUST LAND

PARK BOUNDARY

OVERTON TRAIL

GO JOHN TRAIL

GO JOHN TRAIL

STATE TRUST LAND

PARK BOUNDARY

T START

RAMADA

GO JOHN TRAIL

CLAY MINE TRAIL

STABLES

PARK BOUNDARY

SLATE CREEK TRAIL

FLUME TRAIL

PARK BOUNDARY

PARK BOUNDARY

CAMPING

Entrance $2 FEE

N

SCALE

├─ 1/2 MI ─┤

PARK BOUNDARY

CLOUD

32ND STREET

### LEGEND

PAVED ROAD

DIRT ROAD

SINGLE TRACK

T TRAILHEAD/ PARKING

DANGER (SERIOUS ROUGH STUFF)

PARK BOUNDARY

NEW RIVER ROAD

WASH

TO CA CRE 3 M

TO I-17 CAREFREE ROAD/ CAVE CREEK EXIT 7.4 MILES

CAREFREE HIWAY

CAVE CREEK

TO SCOTTSDALE RD. 2 MILES

TO PHOENIX 20 MILES

# PHOENIX

# Phoenix **CAVE CREEK**
## ONE BURLACIOUS SINGLE TRACK BUTT RUFF

**DISTANCE:** 6.2 MILE LOOP
**TIME:** 1 TO 2 HOURS
**EFFORT:** HEAP O' WORK
**SKILL:** ADVANCED
**PUCK-O-METER:** PUCK 8
  EVIL EXPOSURE & ROCKY DESCENTS
**FIND ROUTE:** FAIRLY EASY
**SEASON:** OCT to MAY

**AT A GLANCE**

3500

**ELEV. (FT.)**

1000

0    **MILES**    20

**DESCRIPTION:** First hork the mondo giganto breakfast burrito at the Jackalope Cafe on Cave Creek Road in Cave Creek then fart your way around this Barny (ultra-Rubble!) loop at Cave Creek Maricopa County Park. Helmet, body armor, full bounce suspension and some goodly tire pressure recommended for this abusive wheel-basher. Other trails down on the flats and on the adjacent State Trust Land aren't quite as hard scrabble.

Surreal views, lotsa great cactus and 6 plus miles of rude, rugged 1-track will challenge and delight any rider with a tough butt, hard head and a death grip on the bars. This is FUN in the most elastic sense of the word. Easily whacked out whiners, weenies and weaklings stay home. Guaranteed to break your Huffy!

You won't need a mileage log. Your computer will probably just pop off and get run over anyway. Mine sure did. Follow the map. I traced it from the county parks' map, so it's pretty right on. There are more trails here, but I have outlined the most obvious loop. Getting lost is not an issue as the terrain is wide open with expansive views and big landmarks.

The park facility includes sparkling bathrooms with TP, picnic area, kiddie playground, ramadas, BBQs and a $2 fee (includes a nifty map) at the gate. Start early AM in summer. October to May is better. Carry a Rambo size camel sack full of $H_2O$. Bring a friend for backup, or better yet, bring an enemy for a good thrashing. Helmet or die!

"Snack on danger. Dine on death."
-mutant credo

**PHOENIX**

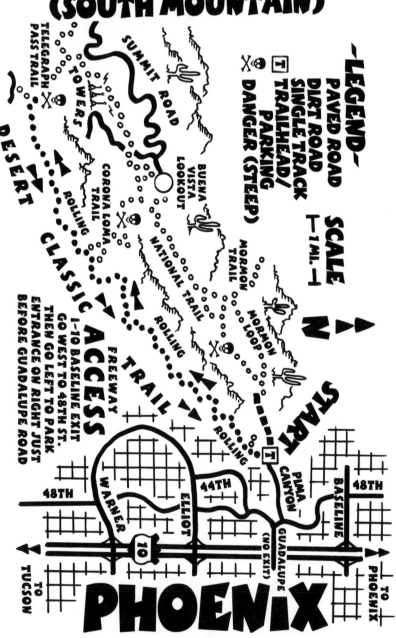

# DESERT CLASSIC
## (SOUTH MOUNTAIN)

DEATH TO COPYCATS!
© 1999
Ⓡ RAY

-LEGEND-

PAVED ROAD
DIRT ROAD
SINGLE TRACK
☠☘ TRAILHEAD/
Ⓣ PARKING
DANGER (STEEP)

SCALE
⊢ 1 MI. ⊣

N

TELEGRAPH PASS TRAIL
TOWERS
SUMMIT ROAD
DESERT
CORONA LOMA TRAIL
ROLLING
BUENA VISTA LOOKOUT
NATIONAL TRAIL
MORMON TRAIL
MORMON LOOP
ROLLING
CLASSIC ACCESS TRAIL
ROLLING
FREEWAY
START

ACCESS:
I-10 BASELINE EXIT
GO WEST TO 48TH ST.
THEN GO LEFT TO PARK
ENTRANCE ON RIGHT JUST
BEFORE GUADALUPE ROAD

48TH
WARNER
ELLIOT
44TH
PIMA-CANYON
GUADALUPE (NO EXIT)
BASELINE
48TH

TO TUCSON
TO PHOENIX
TO PHOENIX

# PHOENIX

# Phoenix DESERT CLASSIC TRAIL
## PRIME SONORAN DESERT SINGLE TRACK

**DISTANCE:** 9 MILES 1-WAY
**TIME:** 2 to 4 HOURS
**EFFORT:** SOME SWEAT
**SKILL:** CHALLENGING FUN
**PUCK-O-METER:** PUCK 7
DEEP WASHES (DANGER IN THE DIPS)
**FIND ROUTE:** EASY
**SEASON:** SEP to MAY

**AT A GLANCE**

3500

**ELEV.
(FT.)**

1000

O  **1-WAY MILES**  9

**DESCRIPTION:** Desert Classic delivers mile after mile of well signed South Mountain single track carve. START south out of the Guadalupe Road lot (see the map). Ahwatulkee on the left, the mountain on your right and dead ahead sets a little line heading off into the giant saguaro. Go hammer. Weekends you can't swing a dead cat without hitting some nig-nog neon poser going way too fast. Watch out on blind cactus corners and use care diving into deep washes. They're double-skull Sid Viscous when the trail comes up to smack you. After about 7 miles out, a short steel post marks a left turn up to the old chopper pad. It's a tough side trip with a good city view. Continue to the end of Desert Classic and return unless you're a glutton. If so, where Desert Classic ends, grunt RIGHT & UP TELEGRAPH PASS TRAIL to NAT'L TRAIL at Summit Road. RIGHT to the Buena Vista parking lot via trail or road and a most excellent descent back down to the Guadalupe Road lot where you started. Add at least 1.5 hours. Whew!

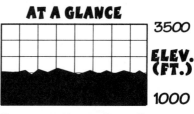

PRIMO

TRAIL

PHOENIX

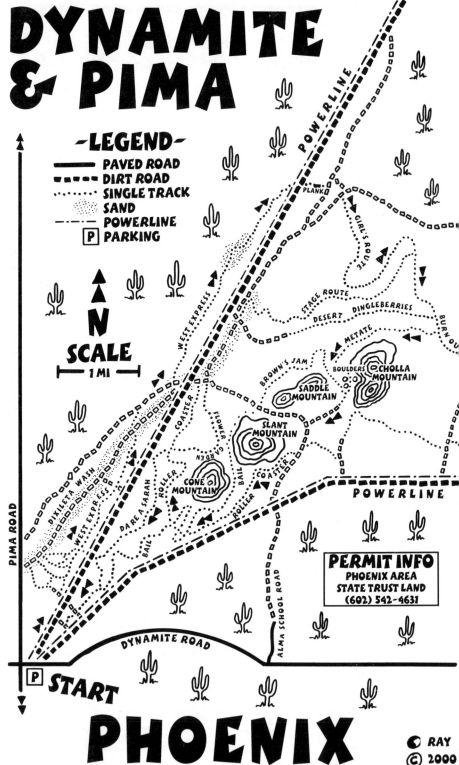

# Phoenix DYNAMITE ROAD
## SUPERB SCOTTSDALE SINGLE TRACK

**DISTANCE:** 1 to 100 MILES
**TIME:** 1 to ? HOURS
**EFFORT:** NOT TOO TOUGH
**SKILL:** EASY TO MODERATE
**PUCK-O-METER:** PUCK 2
GENTLY ROLLING EASY TERRAIN
**FIND ROUTE:** EASY
POWERLINES ARE THE LANDMARKS
**SEASON:** OCT to JUN

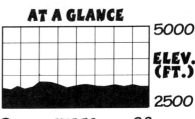

**AT A GLANCE**

5000
ELEV. (FT.)
2500

0          MILES          28

**DESCRIPTION:** Quick, before Phoenix turns into one giant Taco Bell! All available Sonoran desert in the metro area has been gobbled up and will be turned into elegant looking, red tile roof, fake adobe, particle board cracker box. Ouch, Mr. Developer, the truth hurts when you trade desert for dollars.

So, during the last few remaining years, months or days until golf courses consume the planet, shred single track on this state owned land like a boxcar on rails through giant saguaro growing tall along the trails. Though rarely enforced, this state trust land requires a permit for a nominal fee. Call the state land folks at 602-542-2510.

Flowering desert plants light up the routes with neon splashes of color. Trail surfaces are mostly smooth crushed granite with little sand and just beg those G-force carve turns. Tailor your ride to the amount of time available. The map describes a sample loop plus lots of other options and spur trails. START at Dynamite and Pima 8 miles north of Bell Rd. Best in spring, fall and winter. Ride full moon or early AM in summer. Carry lots of agua, major snackage and full kit to bail you out of mechanical trouble if need be.

**PHOENIX**

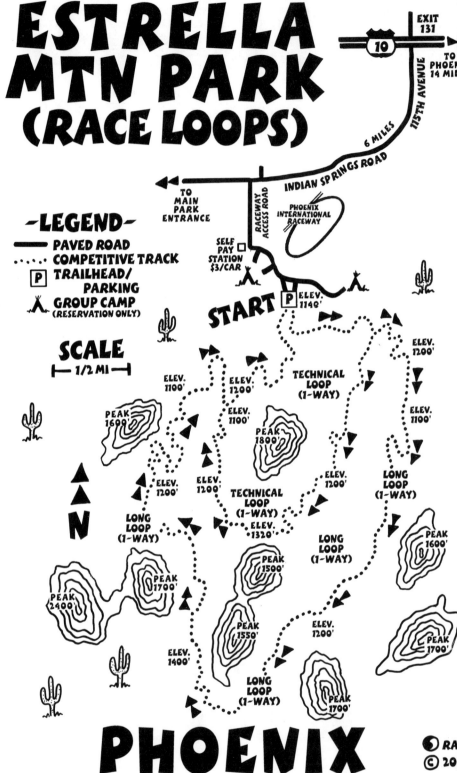

# Phoenix ESTRELLA MOUNTAINS
## 2 HIGH SPEED COMPETITIVE TRACK LOOPS

**DISTANCE:** 13 MI. (2 LOOPS)
**TIME:** 2 HOURS OR SO
**EFFORT:** GOOD WORKOUT
**SKILL:** ADVANCED
  PRACTICE CONTROL AT SPEED
**PUCK-O-METER:** PUCK 7
  SOME FAST TIMES THRU ROUGH JUNK
**FIND ROUTE:** SIGNED
**SEASON:** OCT to MAY

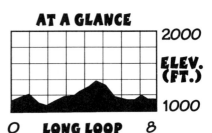

**AT A GLANCE**

2000

**ELEV. (FT.)**

1000

O    **LONG LOOP**    8

**DESCRIPTION:** "The Estrella Mountain Regional Park Competitive Track is for high speeds, challenging one's skills and racing", says Maricopa County Parks and Recreation Department. The track was built with speed in mind. There are two loops, one for speed and the other to hone technical skills. "Even though speed is permitted, there are challenges. Pre-ride the course at a reasonable speed first." I guess that means you can get unreasonable later. "The technical loop is the more difficult. It is for experts only."

"The track is 2 to 8 feet wide. Use the whole cleared width for your own tread and for passing. The track is designed and maintained for skilled users. Do not "improve" it. Do not shortcut. Mud, rocks, sharp curves, etc. are the challenge of the course." Right on. Rocks, curves, mud and ruts! Lots of interesting junk to work around. Bring it on.

The LONG LOOP is 8 miles long. The TECHNICAL LOOP is a total of 5 miles long with a 3 mile technical section. The TECH LOOP is for experts only. The tracks are ONE-WAY going clockwise. See the map. Common sense rules and track etiquette say SLOW RIDERS YIELD TO FASTER RIDERS. Call out before passing. Stay on the designated track. Take extra water and allow extra time. Track closes at sunset. Wear a helmet plus any other protection you might need.

**DIRECTIONS:** Head west out of Phoenix on I-10 toward L.A. for about 14 miles to 115th Ave, EXIT 131. Go south about another 6 miles just past Phoenix International Raceway to the raceway access road on your left. It will cost your car 3 bucks at the self pay station or ride in for one buck each.

"90 % of the game is mental. The other 15% is physical."
  -Yogi Berra

PHOENIX

# RED MOUNTAIN
## (HAWES ROAD)

Ⓢ RAY
Ⓒ 2001

SALT RIVER

GRANITE REEF REC AREA

Ⓟ

JEEP ROAD

0.3

0.4

0.1

CUT ACROSS TRAIL

MINE TRAIL

1.4 MI.

☠

☠

0.6 MI.

0.4 MI.

ENTER MINE TRAIL LOOP

0.8 MI.

RIDGE TRAIL

BIG SAGUARO TRAIL

0.9 MI.

0.9 MI.

☠

N

SADDLEBACK TRAIL

CANAL

0.1

PIG TRAIL

0.8 MI.

0.3

0.3

STORY TRAIL

0.8 MI.

0.7 MI.

POWER ROAD/BUSH HIWAY

C.A.P. CANAL

2.7 MILES

0.5 MI.

1.5 MI.

HAWES TRAIL

TO HAWES ROAD TRAILHEAD (CLOSED)

0.9 MI.

## -LEGEND-

━━━ **PAVED ROAD**
- - - **DIRT ROAD**
····· **SINGLE TRACK**
Ⓟ **PARKING**
☠ **DANGER**
(SERIOUS ROUGH STUFF)

## HAWES ROAD
DEVELOPMENT OF PRIVATE LAND
AT THE END OF HAWES ROAD
HAS CLOSED ACCESS FROM
HAWES ROAD.

## START

Ⓟ

Ⓟ **ALBERTSONS SHOPPING CENTER**

E. McDOWELL ROAD

TO HAWES ROAD (TRAILHEAD CLOSE

SUPERSTITION FREEWAY (HWY 60)
EXIT 188
6 MILES

# PHOENIX (MESA)

# Phoenix (Mesa) RED MOUNTAIN
## KICK ASS LOOP THRU PRISTINE DESERT

**DISTANCE:** 7.1 MILES
**TIME:** 1.5 to 2 HOURS
**EFFORT:** TOUGH
**SKILL:** ADVANCED
**PUCK-O-METER:** PUCK 9
SPEED, EXPOSURE & BOTTOMLESS PIT
**FIND ROUTE:** MODERATE
**SEASON:** OCT to MAY

**AT A GLANCE**

3500

**ELEV. (FT.)**

1000

O  **LOOP MILES**  7.1

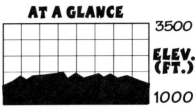

PRIMO TRAIL

PHOENIX

**DESCRIPTION:** The Mine/Hawes Trail Loop just might kick your ass up around your ears and despite the best efforts of greed-head, desert-spoiling, trailhead-closing (Did I forget anything?) developer swine, we still ride the most excellent route in Mesa. Giant saguaro line the paths. Best in cool, wildflower months, there is danger at every turn. Watch for old mine pits just off narrow trails with steep exposure, twisty turning climbs and rapid descents. Yeah baby! I describe my favorite loop, the Hawes/Mine Trail. Get there by heading east from Phoenix out the Superstition Freeway HWY 60 to Power Road then go north to E. McDowell Road.

**PARKING:** Always a real booger at Red Mountain because of private property and smash & grab artists that frequent isolated parking areas. Best bet is to park in the Albertson's lot at McDowell and Power and ride 2.7 miles to the loop trail.

### MILEAGE LOG

0.0 Enter the loop just past the canal bridge on Bush Hwy. See da map. It's an easy paved ride from Albertson's.
0.1 Veer RIGHT onto Pig Trail and climb.
0.9 Continue RIGHT on Hawes Trail and climb some more.
2.4 WAKE UP! Take the LEFT split onto Saddleback Trail.
3.1 Bear RIGHT at Story Trail and continue on Saddleback.
4.0 CAUTION! Mine Trail. Go Right. Wicked rough terrain, high speed and big drops. Careful around old mines.
5.4 LEFT at Cut Across Trail. Some up and down here.
5.8 LEFT on Jeep Road Trail.
6.2 RIGHT at Ridge Trail. More up and down.
7.0 RIGHT at Pig Trail. Almost done.
7.1 Back to Bush Hwy. Whew! Now make up your own loop.

"If you done it, it ain't braggin'."
-some mountain biker dude

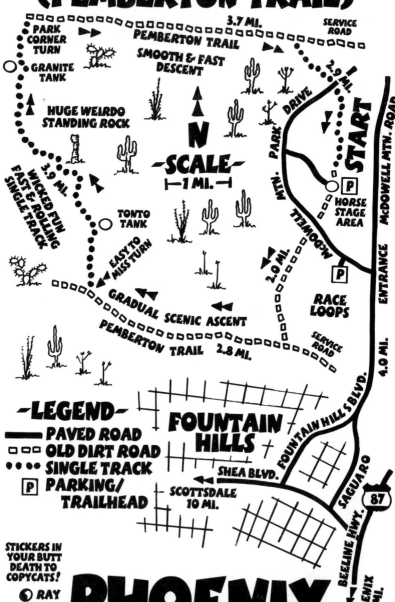

# McDOWELL MOUNTAINS
## (PEMBERTON TRAIL)

PARK CORNER TURN

GRANITE TANK

3.7 MI.

PEMBERTON TRAIL

SERVICE ROAD

SMOOTH & FAST DESCENT

2.9 MI.

START

HUGE WEIRDO STANDING ROCK

MTN. PARK DRIVE

McDOWELL MTN. ROAD

N

SCALE

1 MI.

3.9 MI. WICKED FUN FAST & ROLLING SINGLE TRACK

HORSE STAGE AREA

TONTO TANK

EASY TO MISS TURN

2.0 MI.

GRADUAL SCENIC ASCENT

RACE LOOPS

PEMBERTON TRAIL 2.8 MI.

SERVICE ROAD

McDOWELL

ENTRANCE

4.0 MI.

FOUNTAIN HILLS

FOUNTAIN HILLS BLVD.

SHEA BLVD.

SCOTTSDALE 10 MI.

SAGUARO

87

## LEGEND

—— PAVED ROAD

☐☐☐ OLD DIRT ROAD

•••• SINGLE TRACK

P PARKING/ TRAILHEAD

STICKERS IN YOUR BUTT DEATH TO COPYCATS!

RAY

© 1998

# PHOENIX

BEELINE HWY.

PHOENIX 15 MI.

# Phoenix **McDOWELL MTNS.**
## PEMBERTON SINGLE TRACK LOOP

**DISTANCE:** 15.3 MILE LOOP
**TIME:** 2 HOURS
**EFFORT:** MODERATE
**SKILL:** NOVICE
**PUCK-O-METER:** PUCK 2
FORGIVING, SMOOTH, EASY TERRAIN
**FIND ROUTE:** EASY
**SEASON:** OCT to MAY

**AT A GLANCE**

3500

**ELEV. (FT.)**

1000

O  **LOOP MILES**  15.3

**DESCRIPTION:** You can spy a telephoto view of the McDowells through the purple haze of Phoenix 25 miles away. Quiet, fresh clean air and miles of single track make it seem light years. Excellent, except in 1996 The McDowells were toasted by a (cactus) forest fire. Vegetation has started to recover in earnest. The trails are still there and fun as ever. Now that the new race loops near the park entrance have stolen some of the thunder, Pemberton Trail is still a great alternative if you opt for a less crowded scene. An easy climb up a smooth 2-track is followed by a rip rolling section of single track and ends with a fast 1-track descent. Control speed. This is a multi-use trail. All rules apply. Watch for horsefolk.

**DIRECTIONS:** From Phoenix take the Superstition Freeway HWY 60 east to the Country Club Road exit then north on Country Club as it becomes the Beeline HWY. Continue to Fountain Hills then follow the map to the park entrance. Small entrance fee weekends.

"Amateurs made the ark . Experts made the Titanic."
- Elson Miles

# McDOWELL MOUNTAINS (RACE LOOPS)

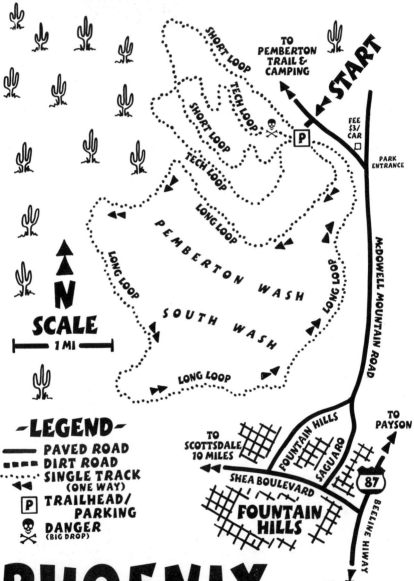

TO PEMBERTON TRAIL & CAMPING

START

SHORT LOOP

TECH LOOP

SHORT LOOP

TECH LOOP

LONG LOOP

PEMBERTON WASH

SOUTH WASH

LONG LOOP

LONG LOOP

LONG LOOP

FEE $3/CAR

PARK ENTRANCE

McDOWELL MOUNTAIN ROAD

N

SCALE

1 MI

## ~LEGEND~

— PAVED ROAD
---- DIRT ROAD
······ SINGLE TRACK (ONE WAY)
◄◄
P TRAILHEAD/PARKING
☠ DANGER (BIG DROP)

TO SCOTTSDALE 10 MILES

FOUNTAIN HILLS

SAGUARO

TO PAYSON

87

SHEA BOULEVARD

FOUNTAIN HILLS

BEELINE HIWAY

TO MESA 15 MILES

© RAY
© 2000

# PHOENIX

# Phoenix MCDOWELL MTNS.
## BIKE RACE (OLD CACTUS CUP) LOOPS

**DISTANCE:** 3 TO 12 MILES
**TIME:** COUPLE OF HOURS?
**EFFORT:** RACE PACE
**SKILL:** EASY TO EXPERT
**PUCK-O-METER:** PUCK 4.5
SOME ROUGH STUFF & ONE BIG DROP
**FIND ROUTE:** NO SWEAT
**SEASON:** OCT to MAY

**AT A GLANCE**

2100

**ELEV. (FT.)**

1600

O     **MILES**     12

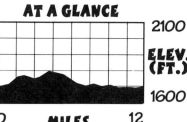

PRIMO

TRAIL

PHOENIX

**DESCRIPTION:** Imagine a place *made* for mountain bikes. The new McDowell Competitive Track is the result of inspiration and hard work by Maricopa County Parks and Rec and many individuals who generously lent of their time and talents. We may ride at race pace on 12 miles of superb new desert trail built and set aside just for mountian bikes.

The terrain is like the old Cactus Cup course at Pinnacle Peak now under (BOO! HISS!) golf course. Remember carving single track like a slot car on speed through a forest of giant saguaro? The Cactus Cup is no more, but this new track is better than ever.

Three single track race loops roll out over this superb desert landscape. A 6-mile LONG LOOP runs up and down all over the prime real estate north of Fountain Hills. A shorter 3-mile SPORT LOOP is challenging and fast while the 3-mile TECH LOOP over T-bone Ridge is guaranteed to peg your personal trick-o-meter. Twisty-turny carving turns, berms, dips, jumps, and roaring fast straightaways . . . it's all here.

Besides race loops, McDowell Mountain Park has miles of other excellent intermediate mountain bike trails, picnic and camping facilities, an expo area and 30 acres of parking. The course is open to the public all year.

**DIRECTIONS:** Located 15 miles northeast of Scottsdale. From Phoenix go east on the Superstition Freeway to Country Club, then north as Country Club becomes Beeline Hiway and continues to Fountain Hills. OR you can go east on Shea to Fountain Hills Blvd. and turn left. There is a nominal $2 per car entrance fee that gets pumped right back into park maintainance and development, so have a couple of bucks in hand.

"Seize the day, put no trust in the 'morrow."
- *ancient poet Horace*
"Seize the day and throttle it."
- *Calvin (Calvin and Hobbs)*

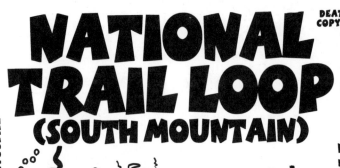

# NATIONAL TRAIL LOOP
## (SOUTH MOUNTAIN)

DEATH TO COPYCATS!

© RAY. 1999

THE TEACHER OF TERROR!

START

TELEGRAPH PASS TRAIL

SUMMIT ROAD

TOWERS

DOWN

DOWN

DOWN

BUENA VISTA LOOKOUT

NATIONAL TRAIL

DANGEROSO DESCENT
(STACKAGE POSSIBLE)

UP

ROLLING

DESERT CLASSIC TRAIL

ROLLING

MORMON TRAIL

MORMON LOOP

UP

UP

UP

~LEGEND~

—— PAVED ROAD

■■■ DIRT ROAD

••••• SINGLE TRACK

T TRAILHEAD

||||| KILLER VIEW

☠ DANGEROSO DESCENT

SCALE
⊢ 1 MI. ⊣

N

FREEWAY ACCESS

I-10 BASELINE EXIT.
GO WEST TO 48TH ST.
THEN GO LEFT TO PARK
ENTRANCE ON RIGHT JUST
BEFORE GUADALUPE ROAD

PIMA CANYON

WARNER

48 TH ST.

ELLIOT

44 TH

GUADALUPE
(NO EXIT)

BASELINE

48TH

10

TO TUCSON

TO PHOENIX

# PHOENIX

# Phoenix NATIONAL TRAIL LOOP
## SOUTH MOUNTAIN TEACHER OF TERROR

**DISTANCE:** 18 MILES
**TIME:** 3 to 4 HOURS
**EFFORT:** SEVERE
**SKILL:** ☠NO BEGINNERS☠
**PUCK-O-METER:** PUCK 10
HAIRY DESCENT PLUS TECH SESSIONS
**FIND ROUTE:** EASY
**SEASON:** SEP to JUN

**AT A GLANCE**

3500

**ELEV. (FT.)**

1000

O  **LOOP MILES**  18

**PRIMO**

**TRAIL**

PHOENIX

**DESCRIPTION:** *Teacher of Terror! Wicked tech tough climb. Narrow single track along a skinny ridge. Ultra hairball, cactus infested descent. Rolling, twisty-turny, 9-mile single track finish. Crackling cat brains! Picture you and Speedmetal skankin' along cliff's edge, brain in neutral, maw of abyss below. Finish up on ripping single track* Desert Classic Trail whoop-de-do rollers that do anything but straight. Weekdays best. Weekends are a freak show. Whilst living so large and quick, kindly consider other trail users. Be polite. Use the big head. HELMET MANDATORY !!!

### MILEAGE LOG

**0.0** START at Guadalupe/Pima Canyon parking lot. See map. Head up the dirt road through gate at west end of lot.

**1.3** Dirt road dead-ends. Trail is down behind "Park Rules" sign on right. GO short quick down then up.

**1.4** Trail splits. Left goes straight up for hard cores. Take the RIGHT (easier UP).

**2.8** LEFT at "T", "Mormon Trail" toward Fat Man's Pass.

**3.6** ARRIVE at Buena Vista Lookout. Continue on National Trail. Caution here. Some hairy exposure as you go down toward the towers. Scary and fast.

**7.5** Sign says Telegraph Pass Trail. Begin the ultra postal psycho descent and don't go over the bars like me!

**9.0** Still with me? CONTINUE LEFT on Desert Classic rollers around the base of mountain on the left and Awatukee on the right. Tour de backyard! Pools and killer mutts over every fence. Where is everybody? Out diggin' up the bucks to feed mutt and mortgage! Very fun, very fast.

**18.0** BACK TO GO. Happy as heck *presuming you lived!*

*"The faster you go, the smoother it gets."*
*- team mutant*

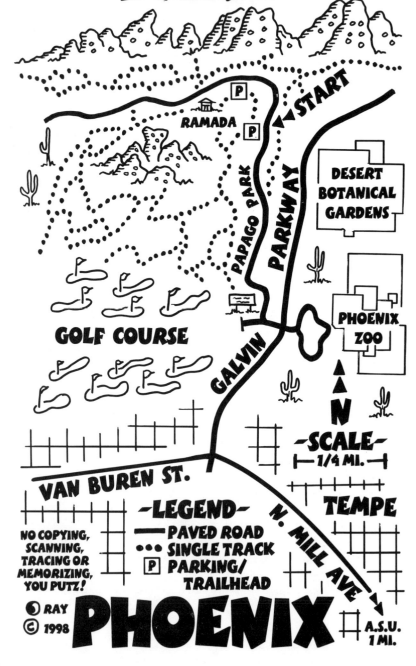

# Phoenix PAPAGO PARK
## EASY FUN SINGLE TRACK LOOPS

**DISTANCE:** 1 TO 5 MILES
**TIME:** 1 TO 2 HOURS
**EFFORT:** EASY
**SKILL:** NOVICE
**PUCK-O-METER:** PUCK O
**FIND ROUTE:** EASY
**SEASON:** ALL YEAR

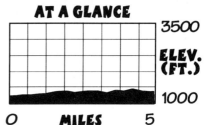

AT A GLANCE

3500

ELEV. (FT.)

1000

0      MILES      5

**DESCRIPTION:** You say to yourself, "Roscoe, this ain't no ride. Too easy." But hey, dude or dudette, don't have an aneurism. This is probably the first place you ever rode dirt in Phoenix. Hundreds of riders do it here every day.

Papago has a lot going for its little self. It's only a mile from ASU. If you're one of the jillion students at that fine institution, it's the only ride you can ride to. Papago is swell for experts and beginners alike. Rookies love the smooth single track trails with just enough woop-de-doos to make life worth living and get a feel for what it's all about. Papago is perfect for the expert who might be pressed for time and can't make it all the way to *The Teacher of Terror* at South Mountain. Just go fast enough, catch enough air and it just doesn't matter where you are. The heart will beat, the head will pound, the feet will smell ... but I digress.

Hear tell Papago is quite agreeable to poach a night ride. Smooth trails, warm temps and a nice bright halogen light add up to some cheap thrills, but you may not park a car in the lot after dark without a hassle. Hey, I never suggest anything illegal. No sir-eee. I merely note that others have done so without regret, so take that for what it's worth. Speaking of regret, the area around The Buttes is reported to be a fave hang for horndogs who can ill afford a room. You'd not be the first night rider to surprise an *au natural* couple *en flagrant*, if you know what I mean. Just be cool as you speed away with a hearty "Hiyo Silver, awaaayyyyy!"

*"It ain't that life is so short, It's just that you're dead so freaking long."*
*-mountain bike wisdom*

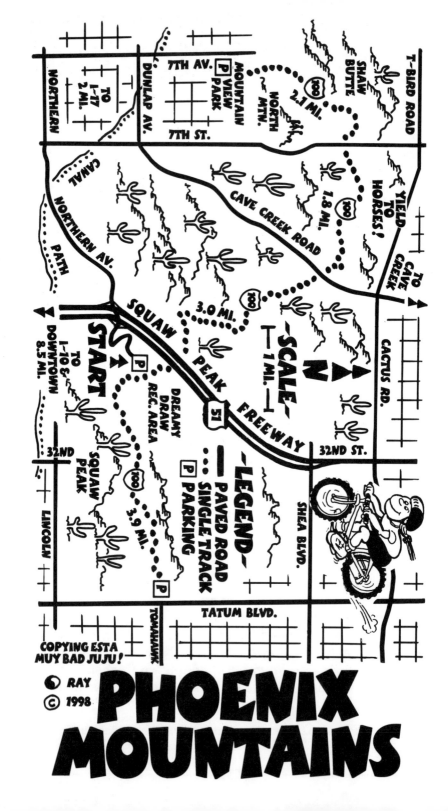

# Phoenix PHOENIX MOUNTAINS
## TRAIL #100 EXCELLENT SINGLE TRACK

**DISTANCE:** 10.7 MILES
**TIME:** 3 to 5 HOURS
**EFFORT:** VERY HARD WORK
**SKILL:** EXPERT
**PUCK-O-METER:** PUCK 7.5
SOME TECHNICAL WORK AND SPEED
**FIND ROUTE:** SIMPLE
**SEASON:** OCT to MAY

**AT A GLANCE**

3000

ELEV.
(FT.)

500

O   1 WAY MILES   10.7

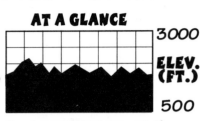

**DESCRIPTION:** Amazes me how you can feel like you're in the middle of a wilderness and yet be right in the heart of the big city. Trail #100 traverses the entire east-west length of the Phoenix Mountains using tunnels under major urban arterials. Making use of the canal path you can complete a nice 20-mile loop doing the whole length of Trail #100 and then return via canal path and a short wicked bit on city streets. See the map. Be very careful on Lincoln.

Clearly marked Trail #100 passes just north of the Dreamy Draw Rec Area parking lot. The westernmost end of Trail #100 might be considered a tad bleak, but the entire rest is excellent with the area east of Dreamy Draw the best for trail and cacti.

**DIRECTIONS:** Access is super easy via HWY 51 Squaw Peak Freeway. Take Northern Av. exit and follow signs to Dreamy Draw Rec Area. This the best place to start. Parking lot on Tatum is dinky. Nearby Valley Cyclery at Cactus and Tatum is a fine shop and a safe car park.

PHOENIX

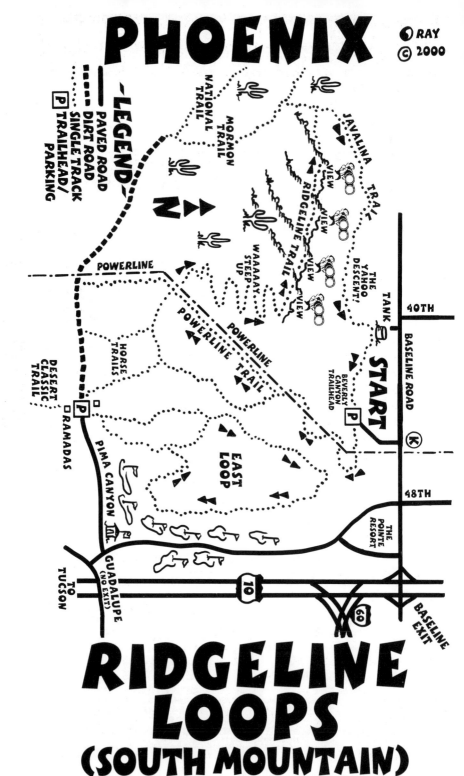

# Phoenix RIDGELINE TRAIL LOOPS
## SECRET SOUTH MOUNTAIN 1-TRACK

**DISTANCE:** 5 to 25 MILES
**TIME:** 2.5 to 5 HOURS
**EFFORT:** TOUGH
**SKILL:** EXPERT
**PUCK-O-METER:** PUCK 8
ROUGH, STEEP DESCENTS
**FIND ROUTE:** TRICKY
**SEASON:** OCT to MAY

**AT A GLANCE**

2000
**ELEV. (FT.)**
1000

O  **LOOP MILES**  5.5

**DESCRIPTION:** TOP SECRET! Most local sprocketheads know dang little about the way cool single track area just north of the main South Mountain Trails, yet these are some of the best. I outline a short tough 5.5 mile loop, but at day's end my odometer read 25 miles to do every great side loop and trail. East Loop is really superb and fairly easy. Everything here is a mix of tough, technical, steep or smooth, but it's all secret single track.

### MILEAGE LOG

0.0  Leave Beverly Cyn. lot on 1-track under power lines. Stay under power lines to avoid false turns.
1.2  Right at Ridgeline Trail sign and steep up over four little peaks and views then zip down to Javelina Trail.
3.1  Right onto Javelina and fast down to reservoir.
4.5  Sharp RIGHT up behind reservoir onto faint 1-track.
5.5  Back to Beverly. Next time try the East Loop.

**PHOENIX**

# UNION HILLS LOOP

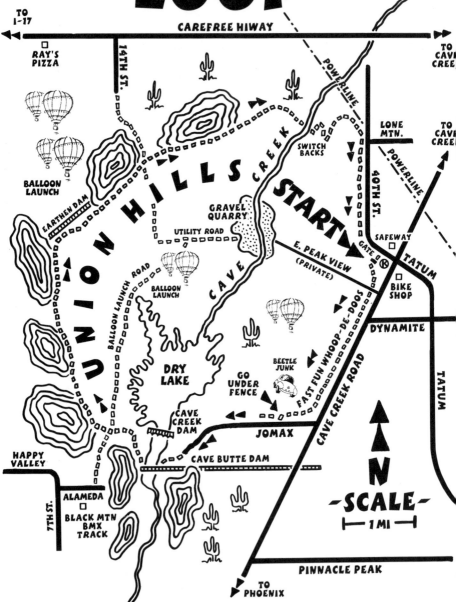

TO
1-17

CAREFREE HIWAY

RAY'S PIZZA

14TH ST.

BALLOON LAUNCH

POWERLINE

TO CAVE CREE

LONE MTN.

TO CAVE CREE

SWITCH BACKS

40TH ST.

POWERLINE

EARTHEN DAM

GRAVEL QUARRY

START

UTILITY ROAD

SAFEWAY

E. PEAK VIEW (PRIVATE)

GATE

TATUM

BALLOON LAUNCH

BALLOON LAUNCH ROAD

CAVE CREEK

BIKE SHOP

DYNAMITE

DRY LAKE

BEETLE JUNK

FAST FUN WHOOP-DE-DOOS

TATUM

GO UNDER FENCE

CAVE CREEK DAM

JOMAX

CAVE CREEK ROAD

N

CAVE BUTTE DAM

SCALE

1 MI

HAPPY VALLEY

7TH ST.

ALAMEDA

BLACK MTN BMX TRACK

PINNACLE PEAK

TO PHOENIX

# PHOENIX

○ RAY

© 1999

# *Phoenix* UNION HILLS LOOP
## VERY FUN, FAST & EASY 18 MILE LOOP

**DISTANCE:** 18 MILES
**TIME:** 2 to 3 HOURS
**EFFORT:** LONG RIDE
**SKILL:** EASY
**PUCK-O-METER:** PUCK O
ZERO PUCKAGE
**FIND ROUTE:** FLAGGED
**SEASON:** SEP to JUN

**AT A GLANCE**

5000

**ELEV. (FT.)**

2500

O　**LOOP MILES**　18

**DESCRIPTION:** Nearly flat, roly-poly, twisting, hopping, jump-ing and way fast loop in North Phoenix. Soil is that superb compacted crushed granite that makes the bitchin' rippin' sound in the turns. It's a wide 2-track ideal for the burning fast middle-to-big-ring training loop or a non-technical, longish dirt ride for the beginner. The trail surface is just challenging enough with dips, hops and bumps to make it *NOT* a total putz ride. Early weekend mornings are best to catch the dozens of balloons that launch here and to avoid the heat.

Union Hills Loop is Arizona State Trust land. Although not strictly enforced, you need a permit to ride here. Said permits are available from the state at (602) 542-2510 or pick one up at Spokesman Bike Shop near the START at Cave Creek and Tatum. There is a nominal fee that gets you in the club and allows you to ride legal beagle style on the superb trails around Dynamite & Pima. The groovy guys at Spokesman have been kind enough to flag the route so you won't get lost. Stop in and say thanks. Tell 'em Ray sent ya.

**PHOENIX**

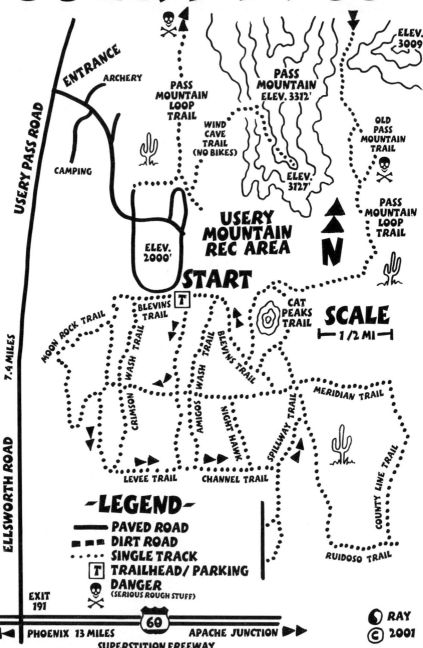

# USERY PASS

PHOENIX (MESA)

# *Phoenix* USERY MOUNTAIN PARK
## SONORAN DESERT SINGLE TRACK

**DISTANCE:** 5 & 8 MILE LOOPS
**TIME:** 2 to 4 HOURS
**EFFORT:** NO SWEAT
**SKILL:** CHALLENGING FUN
**PUCK-O-METER:** PUCK 5
(Some puck 10 on the long loop)
**FIND ROUTE:** DARN EASY
**SEASON:** SEP to MAY

**AT A GLANCE**

3500

**ELEV. (FT.)**

1000

O    **LOOP MILES**    4.7
      (BLEVINS LOOP)

**DESCRIPTION:** Named for King Usery, a rancher in the 1890s. Ranching went sour. King tried robbing the Globe-Florence stage with pal Bill Blevins. Posse tracked them here to Usery Ranch. Two years later King was pardoned the rest of his seven years from Yuma territorial pen. Next, Mr. King takes up horse borrowing. Gets time back in Yuma. After release he vanished. Necktie party no doubt.

     This pristine sonoran desert is best enjoyed in cooler months October to May or veeery early AM during summer inferno. The Superstitions are to the east. The Userys are just north and the McDowells sit across the Salt River northwest. Up close is Pass Mountain.

**BLEVINS LOOP TRAIL**, called "Usery Loves Company" by the local wig-wags, is a perfect easy to moderate 4.7 mile single track carve for the beginner to intermediate rider. It is signed and has virtually zero elevation gain. Great for easy exploration with no possibility of getting lost.

**PASS MOUNTAIN LOOP** is more of a real deal kinda ride. Tough 8 mile single track, rocky washes and sick twisted fun for the more seasoned rider. Starts off easy but gets tough quick once behind Pass Mountain. No water. No rescue.

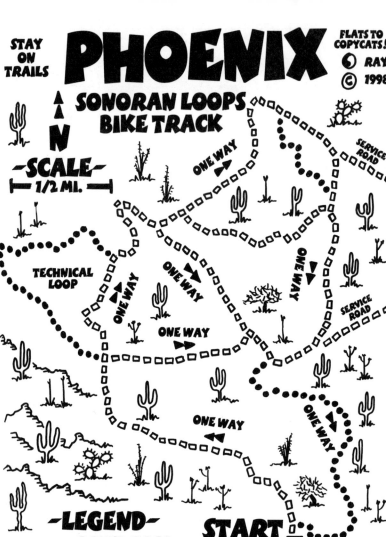

# PHOENIX

STAY ON TRAILS

FLATS TO COPYCATS!
🌙 RAY
© 1998

## SONORAN LOOPS BIKE TRACK

↑ N

-SCALE-
⊢ 1/2 MI.

SERVICE ROAD

ONE WAY ▶

TECHNICAL LOOP

ONE WAY ▶

ONE WAY ▶

ONE WAY ▶

ONE WAY ▶▶

SERVICE ROAD

ONE WAY ◀

ONE WAY ▶

-LEGEND-

━━━ PAVED ROAD

▢▢▢▢ OLD 2-TRACK DIRT ROAD

•••• SINGLE TRACK

[P] PARKING/ TRAILHEAD

**START**

[P]

1 MI.

ENTRANCE

OLIVE/ DUNLAP

TO PHOENIX 15 MI. ▶▶

COTTON/ 171 ST AV.

TO I-10 EXIT 124

# WHITE TANK MOUNTAINS

# Phoenix WHITE TANK MTNS.
## EASY 1-TRACK AND JEEP ROAD LOOPS

**DISTANCE:** 5.6 MILE LOOP
**TIME:** 1 HOUR OR SO
**EFFORT:** EASY
**SKILL:** NOVICE
**PUCK-O-METER:** PUCK 2
EASY ROLLING TERRAIN, NO ALARM
**FIND ROUTE:** EASY
**SEASON:** OCT to MAY

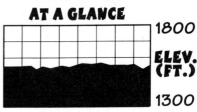

**AT A GLANCE**

1800

**ELEV. (FT.)**

1300

O  **LOOP MILES**  5.6

**DESCRIPTION:** "SONORAN LOOP TRAIL: MOUNTAIN BIKE DIFFICULTY MODERATE" reads the sign at the trailhead. Situated 15 miles due west of Peoria strip malls and traffic, Sonoran Loop is fairly flat, easy and nestled up against the base of the extremely rugged White Tank Mountains. Sonoran desert, fresh air, open sky and glorious silence replenish the soul . . . guaranteed. The White Tanks are best in cool months when the desert blooms. Cloudy, cool skies are ideal.

Interesting to note that novice friends and family won't hate you for dragging them here. Easy jeep roads and level rolling single track with a few short excursions across sandy washes. A great place to get your trail legs going and improve wind and skills. Also, Maricopa County has recently done a great job improving the single track, connecting loose ends and closing heinously rough, rocky jeep roads that headed steep up into nowhere.

**CAUTION:** Mr. Western Diamondback Rattler resides here. He is one mean machine. Adults grow to 7 feet, have a heavy body with dark, diamond shaped spots and are unmistakable when aroused. Do not mess with! Observe from a distance. Only dangerous when come upon suddenly. He wishes you to leave him alone which is his right as a southwest native since before time and Arizona.

**DIRECTIONS:** Located 15 miles west of Peoria at the west end of Olive (Dunlap) Ave. Quicker access is via I-10 west all the way to Cotton Ave. (exit 124), north 7 miles to Olive and then 5 miles west to the park entrance.

"The more I know people, the more I like my bike."
-anonymous bike mechanic

**PHOENIX**

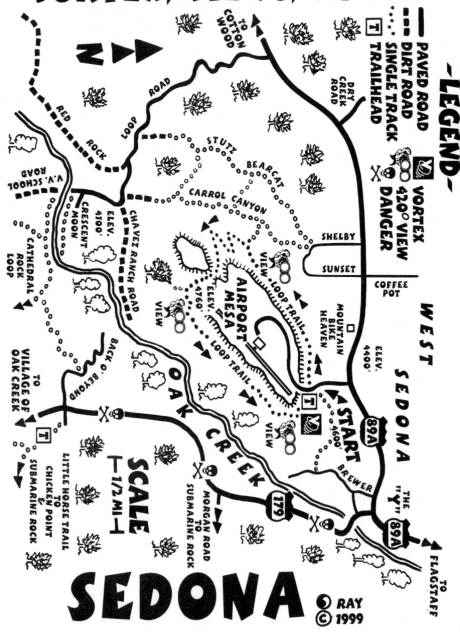

# AIRPORT MESA LOOP
## VORTEX, VIEWS, ABUSE

-LEGEND-

PAVED ROAD
DIRT ROAD
SINGLE TRACK
TRAILHEAD
VORTEX
420° VIEW
DANGER

N

TO COTTONWOOD

DRY CREEK ROAD

RED ROCK LOOP ROAD

LOOP ROAD

STUTZ BEARCAT

CARROL CANYON

V.V. SCHOOL ROAD

CRESCENT MOON

ELEV. 4100'

CHAVEZ RANCH ROAD

SHELBY

SUNSET

COFFEE POT

CATHEDRAL ROCK LOOP

VIEW LOOP TRAIL

AIRPORT MESA

ELEV. 4760'

MOUNTAIN BIKE HEAVEN

ELEV. 4400'

WEST SEDONA

TO VILLAGE OF OAK CREEK

BACK O' BEYOND

OAK CREEK

VIEW

LOOP TRAIL

ELEV. 4600'

START

89A

THE "Y"

LITTLE HORSE TRAIL TO CHICKEN POINT & SUBMARINE ROCK

SCALE 1/2 MI.

MORGAN ROAD TO SUBMARINE ROCK

179

BREWER

89A

TO FLAGSTAFF

## SEDONA

RAY
© 1999

# *Sedona* AIRPORT MESA LOOP
## ROUGH STUFF QUICKIE WITH MEGA VIEWS

**DISTANCE:** 3.5 MILES
**TIME:** 1 TO 2 HOURS
**EFFORT:** PRETTY TOUGH
**SKILL:** PICANTE
**PUCK-O-METER:** PUCK 7
**FIND ROUTE:** EASY
**SEASON:** SEP to JUN

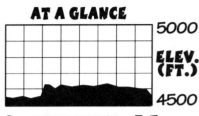

**AT A GLANCE**

5000

**ELEV. (FT.)**

4500

O    **LOOP MILES**    3.5

**DESCRIPTION:** "This is *NOT* a ride!", your homies will holler, but they be wrong. It *is* rough, physical, abusive and in short, perfect, at least for most Canadians worth their Molson. However, the trail is short without much climbing once you are up on the mesa, so not *that* bad.

A rocky, well defined loop circumnavigates the rim 600 feet above town. As you go around, you have killer views in every direction. It's a great test for your full suspension machine and your technical skills.

**DIRECTIONS:** Easy. Best bet is to park at Mountain Bike Heaven bike shop. See the map. From HWY 89A, head up Airport Road. The vortex parking area and lots of tourists are on the left. The trail starts directly across the road behind the guardrail.

"Life is not a journey to the grave with the intention of arriving safely in one pretty and well preserved piece, but to skid broadside, thoroughly used up, worn out and shouting GERONIMO!!!"
- Nod, (G)Narly Old Dude

# WWW.MOUNTAINBIKEHEAVEN.COM

SEDONA

# BOYNTON PASS

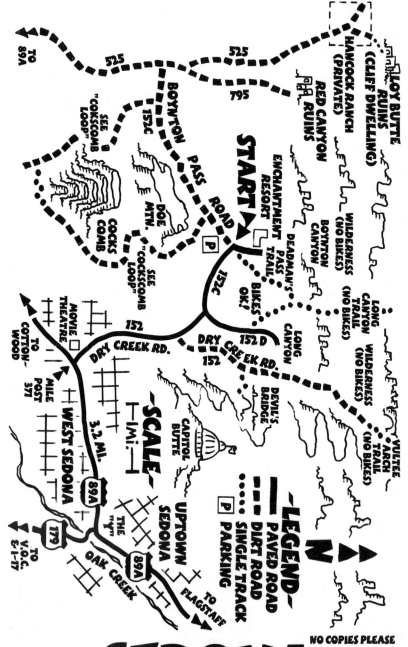

# SEDONA

© 1997
 RAY

# *Sedona* BOYNTON PASS ROAD
## EASY DIRT ROAD TO RUIN(S)

**DISTANCE:** 20 MILES
**TIME:** 3 to 4 HOURS
**EFFORT:** LONG EASY ROLL
**SKILL:** NOT MUCH NEEDED
**PUCK-O-METER:** PUCK 2
SOME CARS ON DIRT ROAD
**FIND ROUTE:** EASY
**SEASON:** SEP to MAY

**AT A GLANCE**

4600

**ELEV. (FT.)**

4200

O     **MILES**     20

**DESCRIPTION:** Red dirt roads and gentle climbs roll through pinon and juniper with the red rock buttes of Secret Mountain Wilderness overhead. Ancient ruins, optional hikes and patented technicolor Sedona scenes make this an unforgettable day.

### LOY BUTTE

It's fairly smooth dirt road to the ruins, although you car might not think so. PARK where FS 152C turns dirt (see map). CONTINUE 4 miles to FS 525 and turn RIGHT. After 0.1 miles BEAR LEFT and go 3 miles to Hancock Ranch and Loy Butte. Go straight through the ranch and stay on the road.

Do not disturb the ruins. Do not pick up anything. Do not touch the petroglyphs. Dirt and oil from many hands over time do great damage. Think about the time before time and those who lived here then. Avoid dusty tourist traffic. Ride early. Carry food, water and kit.

### RED CANYON

Same directions as Loy Butte only BEAR RIGHT on FS 525 onto FS 795. Then it's 2 miles out to the ruins all on smooth dirt road. Enjoy the ruins with your eyes only. Do not pick up or disturb any artifacts you may find. Do not ride close to the ruin.

**NOTE:** It is said that the 5000 or so archeological sites around Sedona are protected not only by law, but also by evil curse. No joke. Do not be so foolish as to tempt the ancients with bad ju-ju. Respect those who have gone before you. They may be waiting in the next life!

*"As far as possible without surrender be on good terms with all."*
*- popular wisdom*

SEDONA

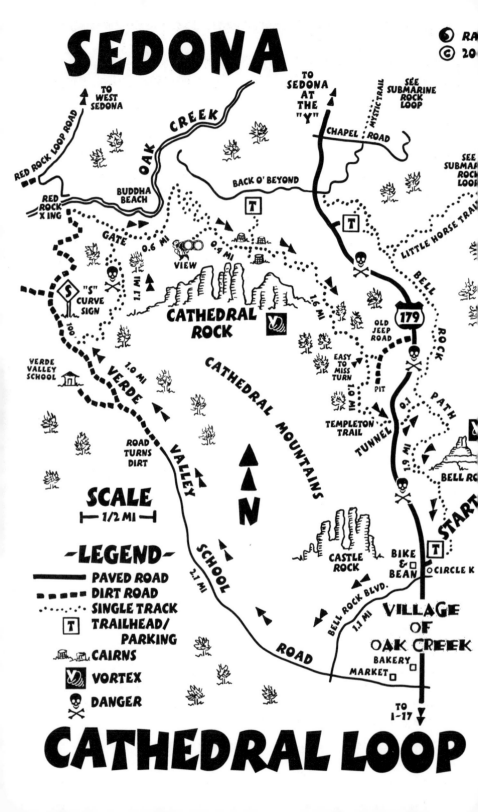

# *Sedona* CATHEDRAL ROCK LOOP
## SINGLE TRACK VIA BUDDHA BEACH

**DISTANCE:** 10.9 MILES
**TIME:** 2 HOURS OR SO
**EFFORT:** MODERATE
**SKILL:** ADVANCED
**PUCK-O-METER:** PUCK 7
SOME SPEED AND EXPOSURE
**FIND ROUTE:** MODERATE
**SEASON:** SEP to JUN

**AT A GLANCE**

4500

**ELEV. (FT.)**

4000

O   **LOOP MILES**   10.9

**DESCRIPTION:** Cathedral Rock/Buddha Beach Loop has it all. Views, slickrock, single track AND a swimming hole. After a short paved warm up, hop on a technical rolling 1-track to the creek. Climb up steep from the creek then follow an excellent very scenic trail around the contour of picturesque Cathedral Rock. Cross UNDER busy HWY 179 to Bell Rock Path and jam around Bell Rock back The Village.

PRIMO TRAIL

## MILEAGE LOG

0.0  START near Circle K in Village of Oak Creek. Follow the map to just before the "S"curve sign on Verde Valley School Rd.

4.2  RIGHT about 100 ft. before "S" curve sign and onto very fun 1-track technical rollers to Oak Creek.

5.3  RIGHT at gate thru fence to Oak Creek and Buddha Beach just across. Swimming hole with rope is a welcome sight on a hot day. The trail CONTINUES upstream thru boulders on hill above creek then down along shore.

5.8  RIGHT and WAY STEEP UP. UGH!

5.9  SUMMIT VIEW. Bear LEFT. Trail leads south along the contour face of Cathedral Rock. STAY ON MAIN TRAIL.

6.3  CROSS main Cathedral hiking trail marked by big rock cairns. You CONTINUE STRAIGHT on MAIN TRAIL. Trail soon winds down into the pinon and juniper trees.

7.9  BE ALERT! Many main trail tire tracks follow obvious, but easy-to-miss single track to the RIGHT. May or may not be marked with cairns. Leads to tunnel and safe crossing.

8.9  TUNNEL under HWY 179. Continue up to the left.

9.0  Bell Rock Path. Go RIGHT. Path leads around Bell Rock and back down to The Village. Watch for hikers here.

10.9 Back to Trailhead and tourists. Head down to Desert Flour Bakery (see map) for major java/snackage.

**SEDONA**

# COCKSCOMB LOOP

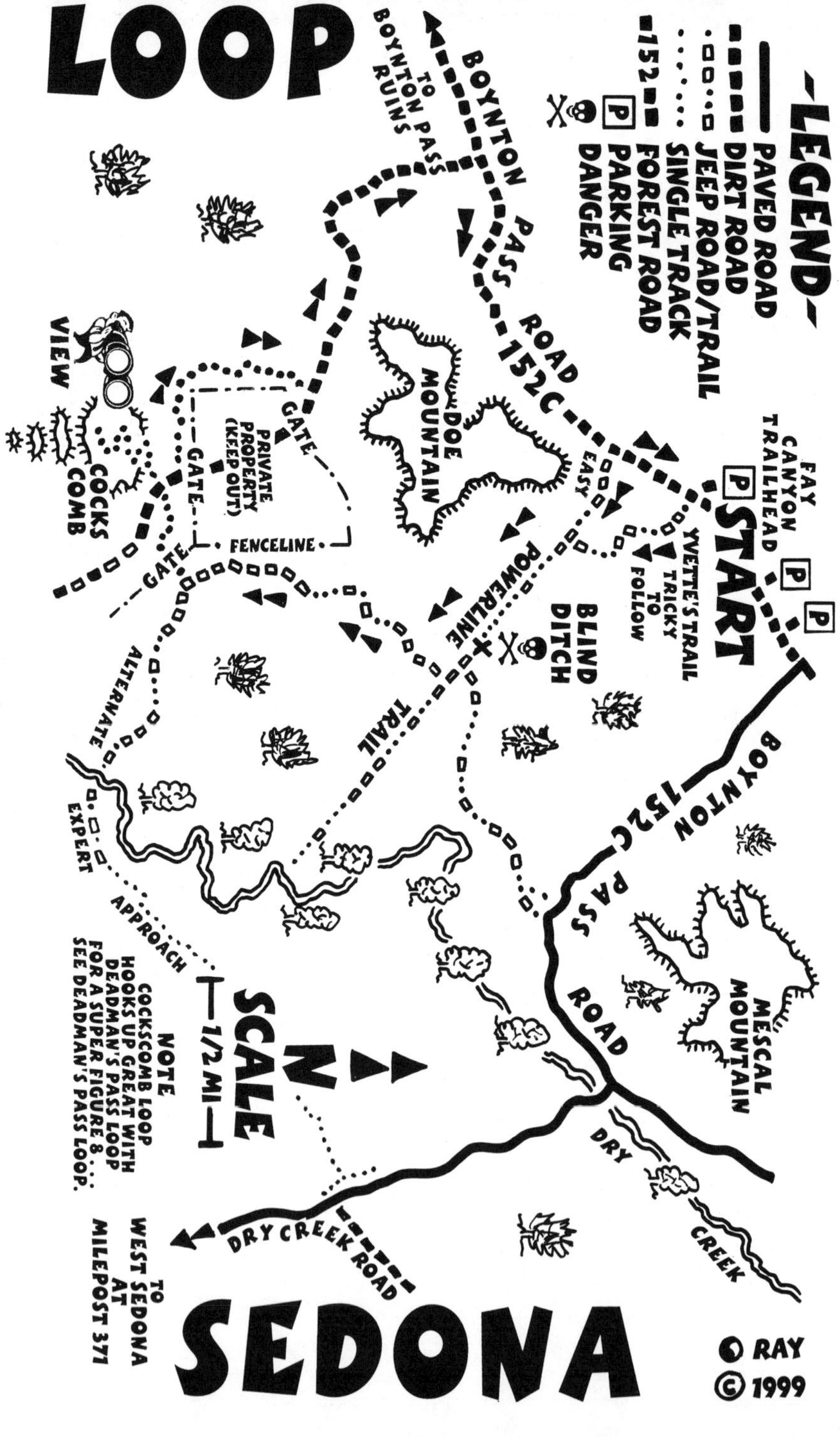

## — LEGEND —

- ▬▬▬ PAVED ROAD
- ■ ■ ■ DIRT ROAD
- ◻ ◻ ◻ JEEP ROAD/TRAIL
- • • • • SINGLE TRACK
- ■■■■ FOREST ROAD
- P PARKING
- ☠✗ DANGER
- 152

TO BOYNTON RUINS

BOYNTON PASS

BOYNTON PASS ROAD 152C

DOE MOUNTAIN

VIEW

COCKS COMB

GATE
GATE
GATE
PRIVATE PROPERTY (KEEP OUT)
FENCELINE

EASY

FAY CANYON TRAILHEAD

P START P P

YVETTE'S TRAIL
TRICKY TO FOLLOW

BLIND DITCH

POWERLINE TRAIL

☠✗

ALTERNATE APPROACH
EXPERT

N
SCALE
1/2 MI

BOYNTON 152C PASS ROAD

MESCAL MOUNTAIN

NOTE
COCKSCOMB LOOP
HOOKS UP GREAT WITH
DEADMAN'S PASS LOOP
FOR A SUPER FIGURE 8.
SEE DEADMAN'S PASS LOOP.

DRY CREEK

DRY CREEK ROAD

TO WEST SEDONA AT MILEPOST 371

# SEDONA

© RAY
© 1999

# *Sedona* **COCKSCOMB LOOP**
## BIG FUN TRAIL TO SEDONA SPIRES

**DISTANCE:** 6.1 MILES
**TIME:** 1 to 2 HOURS
**EFFORT:** MEDIUM WORK
**SKILL:** NOT TOO TRICKY
**PUCK-O-METER:** PUCK 6
BEWARE THE ONE EVIL BLIND DITCH
**FIND ROUTE:** BIT TRICKY
**SEASON:** SEP to JUN

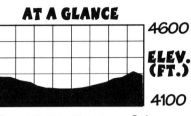

**AT A GLANCE**

4600

**ELEV. (FT.)**

4100

0   **LOOP MILES**   6.1

**DESCRIPTION:** Cockscomb's red spires invite you like a redrock Emerald City of OZ as you cruise west thru Sedona. Ride the red dirt to the base then scramble up top on foot for the best 420 degree view in these parts.

### MILEAGE LOG

0.0 Follow the map and find your way to the Fay Canyon Trailhead on Boynton Pass Road. The loop begins just across the road from the parking lot.

0.3 Connect with Powerline Trail. Go LEFT and down.

1.0 HEADS UP! Bad Blind Ditch! RIGHT turn coming up.

1.2 RIGHT first chance after the Blind Ditch hazard and head away from the Powerline Trail on another old jeep road double track/single track trail.

2.1 You come upon a fence and an area of deciduous trees. Take single track on RIGHT thru gate in fence.

2.4 The 1-track crosses a jeep road. Continue straight on the trail for a bit then stash your bike, but don't forget where you left it. You may need it later. Continue up the steep trail on foot. It leads you to the top of The Cockscomb, a spire 400 feet off the pinon and juniper deck. Cairns mark the way. After the view session return to the jeep road. There is a big steel gate in the fence. Don't go thru it. A single track leads along the fence. See the map.

3.1 Go LEFT on the big gravel road.

4.1 Boynton Pass Road. Go RIGHT back to the Start.

6.1 Back to GO. Now, if not too pooped out, turn these pages to Deadman's Pass Loop and double your fun with a bitchin' little figure-8 double loop.

**SEDONA**

# DEADMAN'S PASS LOOP

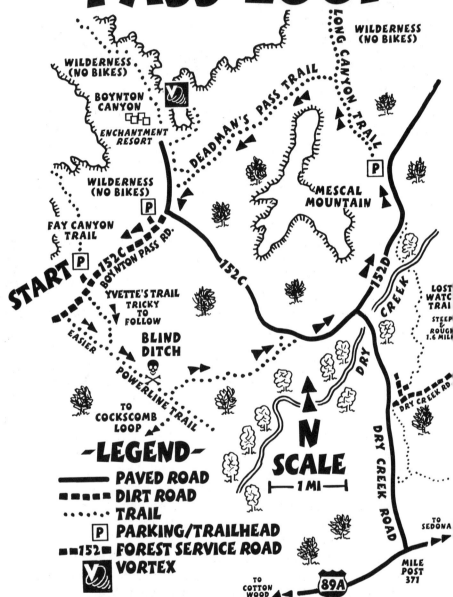

WILDERNESS (NO BIKES)

LONG CANYON TRAIL

WILDERNESS (NO BIKES)

BOYNTON CANYON

ENCHANTMENT RESORT

DEADMAN'S PASS TRAIL

MESCAL MOUNTAIN

P

WILDERNESS (NO BIKES)

FAY CANYON TRAIL

P

START

152C

BOYNTON PASS RD.

152C

152D

CREEK

LOST WATC TRAI

STEEP & ROUGH 1.6 MIL

YVETTE'S TRAIL TRICKY TO FOLLOW

BLIND DITCH

EASIER

POWERLINE TRAIL

DRY

DRY CREEK RD

TO COCKSCOMB LOOP

## -LEGEND-

| | |
|---|---|
| ——— | PAVED ROAD |
| ▪▪▪▪▪ | DIRT ROAD |
| •••••• | TRAIL |
| P | PARKING/TRAILHEAD |
| ▪152▪ | FOREST SERVICE ROAD |
| V | VORTEX |

N

SCALE

1 MI

DRY CREEK ROAD

TO SEDONA

MILE POST 371

TO COTTON WOOD

89A

# SEDONA

# *Sedona* DEADMAN'S PASS LOOP
## QUICK FUN SINGLE TRACK LOOP

**DISTANCE:** 6.4 MILE LOOP
**TIME:** 1 HOUR
**EFFORT:** MODERATE
**SKILL:** INTERMEDIATE
**PUCK-O-METER:** PUCK 7
  BLIND DITCH AND FAST DESCENTS
**FIND ROUTE:** JUST A BIT
  TRICKY AT FIRST
**SEASON:** SEP to JUN

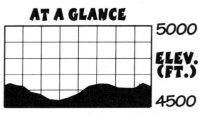

**AT A GLANCE**

5000

**ELEV.
(FT.)**

4500

O   **LOOP MILES**   6.4

**DESCRIPTION:** Kicks off with a red dirt, wicked fun single track line down an old powerline 2-track. Lots of rolling drops and dips. Watch out for the Blind Ditch! Head back up a combination of dirt trail and a short paved bit. Finally, rock and roll down Deadman's Pass Trail behind Mescal Mountain for your daily crazy fun fix. Don't forget to check out Boynton Canyon Vortex. It lives at the foot of Kachina Woman formation at the entrance to Boynton Canyon. See the map. Follow the tourists.

Want more? Deadman's Pass Loop links up nicely with six-mile Cockscomb Loop for a mighty fine figure 8.

### MILEAGE LOG

0.0 Check out the map and make your way to the START at Fay Canyon Trailhead on Boynton Pass Road. The trail begins just across the road from the parking lot. It's not too tricky if you follow the bike tracks.

0.3 Connect with Powerline Trail. Go LEFT and down.

1.0 LOOKOUT! Blind Ditch! Your left turn is coming up.

1.1 Go LEFT. More rollers and fun stuff while connecting back to paved Boynton Pass Road.

2.1 Boynton Pass Road pavement. Go RIGHT.

2.7 Continue LEFT onto Long Canyon Road FS 152D.

3.3 Long Canyon Trailhead on LEFT. Take it.

4.3 LEFT onto signed Deadman's Pass Trail. Hold on!

5.7 Pavement. Boynton Canyon Road. See the map. Look for tourists looking for the vortex. Impress them with the knowledge that it resides beneath the Kachina Woman. Now LEFT back to Boynton Pass.

5.8 Unpaved Boynton Pass Road. CONTINUE.

6.4 Back to go at Fay Canyon Trailhead parking lot. Now flip the page back to Cockscomb Loop and go do it.

# HUCKABY LOOP

-LEGEND-

— PAVED ROAD
- - - - DIRT ROAD
...... TRAIL
[P] PARKING/TRAILHEAD
☠ DANGER
✗ (BIG DROPS)

STEAMBOAT ROCK

JIM

THOMPSON TRAIL

WILSON CANYON TRAIL

MIDGLEY BRIDGE [P]

GATE [P]

JORDAN TRAIL TO SOLDIERS PASS & DRY CREEK ROAD

JORDAN ROAD

N

89A

THE STAIRS

OAK CREEK

HUCKABY TRAIL

UPTOWN SEDONA

THE "Y"

89A

TO WEST SEDONA

SEDONA SPORTS

179

BEAR WALLOW CANYON

[P]

SCHNEBLY HILL ROAD

START

TO VILLAGE OF OAK CREEK & I-17

SEDONA

# *Sedona* HUCKABY TRAIL LOOP
## TOUGH SCENIC LOOP ALONG OAK CREEK

**DISTANCE:** 8.5 MILES
**TIME:** 1.5 TO 3 HOURS
**EFFORT:** HARD
**SKILL:** EXPERT
**PUCK-O-METER:** PUCK 9
WICKED EXPOSURE, BIG DROPS, STAIRS
**FIND ROUTE:** SIGNED
**SEASON:** SEP to JUN

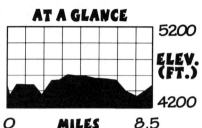

**AT A GLANCE**

5200

**ELEV. (FT.)**

4200

0    **MILES**    8.5

**DESCRIPTION:**  Very fun from the get-go down rough, winding single track into Bear Wallow Canyon and back up the other side.  Follows along above Oak Creek often on cliff's edge. Great views if you dare look. Down the stairs from hell to the creek for a double wet crossing then up to Midgley Bridge. Head up Wilson Canyon Trail and over rough as heck Jim Thompson Trail before downhill finish.

### NOTE: THIS LOOP NOT POSSIBLE DURING HIGH WATER IN OAK CREEK . . . INQUIRE LOCALLY.

### MILEAGE LOG

0.0 START at parking lot on left just as paved Schnebly Hill Road turns dirt. Trail begins at lower end of open area below the paved parking lot. Huckaby crosses Bear Wallow Canyon then back up along cliffs above the creek. Beware big drops and The Stairs just before the creek.

1.8 Cross Oak Creek, cross again then climb up steep switchbacks to Midgley Bridge.

2.6 Cross the parking lot and head up Wilson Canyon Trail . Trail  crosses dry Wilson Creek and soon meets the sign for Jim Thompson Trail.

3.3 Grind uphill  as Jim Thompson  single track finds its way  leading up through rocky climb.

3.6 Go RIGHT when Jim Thompson meets a short loop.

6.0 LEFT when Jim Thompson meets a gravel road then take pavement through Sedona back to GO.

8.5 Back to go on Schnebly Hill Road.

SEDONA

# *Sedona* BELL ROCK LOOPS
## WAY FUN ROOKIE SINGLE TRACK

**DISTANCE:** 3 MILE LOOP
(MORE IF YOU WANT)
**TIME:** 1 to 2 HOURS
**EFFORT:** FAIRLY EASY
**SKILL:** NOT VERY TOUGH
(AS EASY AS SEDONA GETS)
**PUCK-O-METER:** PUCK 4
**FIND ROUTE:** EASY
**SEASON:** SEP to JUN

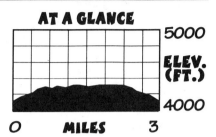

AT A GLANCE

5000

ELEV.
(FT.)

4000

O    MILES    3

**DESCRIPTION:** Humongo views and patented superb Sedona single track with redrock monuments Bell Rock and Courthouse Butte towering overhead. You can't get lost if you just look up. The trails are fun and fast, hard-pack grippy soil with just enough moderate technical challenges to make you break a sweat. Great practice.

Bell Rock Path is the "launch ramp" to single track on both sides of HWY 179. Seasoned riders will zoom up to Submarine Rock Loop, Llama Loop or tunnel under HWY 179 to Cathedral Rock Loop and Buddha Beach.

NOTE: Follow the map, but do NOT follow Courthouse Loop over the saddle behind Courthouse Rock. That short part of Courthouse Loop is tempting but for hikers only as it peaks out above 4400' elevation and is thus wilderness. No bikes allowed. $300 fine! Serious.

**DIRECTIONS:** Take I-17 exit 298 to the Village of Oak Creek. Park in the Bell Rock Pathway parking lot on HWY 179 across from the Bike & Bean and next to the Circle K.

SEDONA

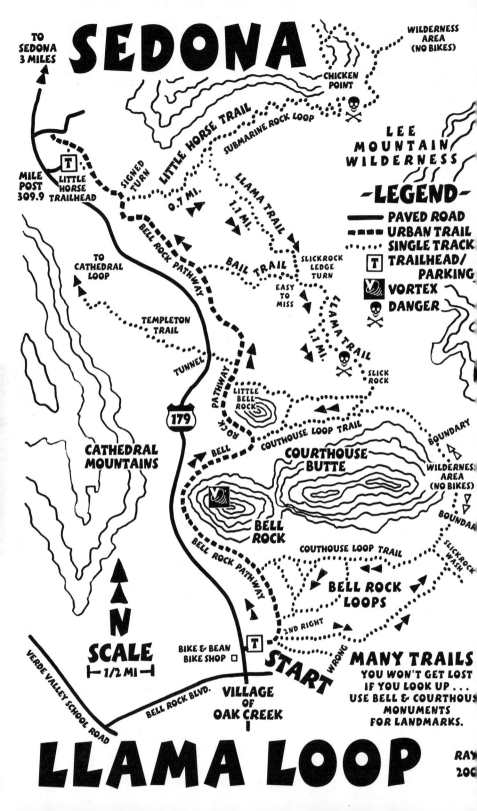

# *Sedona* LLAMA TRAIL LOOP
## WICKED FUN SEDONA SINGLE TRACK

**DISTANCE:** 8 MILE LOOP
(EASIER LOOPS NEARBY)

**TIME:** 2 TO 2.5 HOURS

**EFFORT:** HARD

**SKILL:** SERIOUS

**PUCK-O-METER:** PUCK 8

**FIND ROUTE:** NOT EASY
(ODOMETER WOULD BE HELPFUL)

**SEASON:** SEP to JUN

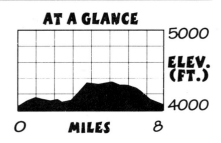

AT A GLANCE

5000

ELEV. (FT.)

4000

0       MILES       8

**DESCRIPTION:** If you could pop Llama Loop into a DVD player, you might term it a "riotous, edgy thriller". Killer views and twisty-fast-then-suddenly-technical single track are its trademark. Carvy slotcar turns become suddenly technical enough to make life thrilling. The trick-o-meter sits mid-way between seasoned and expert.

Redrock monuments Bell and Courthouse tower overhead. Catch postcard glimpses of Cathedral Rock, Thumb Butte, Twin Buttes, Rabbit Ears and even Cockscomb's spires way far in the purple distance. You can't get lost if you just look up at the monumental faces of Bell and Courthouse. Learn them.

Llama Trail is not a "system" trail, not on any other map and thus fabulously not "improved". It is just below that magic 4400' elevation contour making it non-wilderness and thus legal. It is the higher, gnarlier and parallel twin to the sonorous Bell Rock Pathway urban trail. Llama separates serious and often high speed, thrill seeker bike traffic from urban trail rookies and tourist foot traffic. It is unmarked. An odometer will come in very handy. If your navigation skills are weak, skip it. If you do it, STAY ON THE TRAIL. STAY OUT OF THE WILDERNESS. $300 fine for wilderness area violations!

**DIRECTIONS:** Take I-17 exit 298 to the Village of Oak Creek. Park in Bell Rock Pathway urban trail lot on HWY 179 next to the Circle K. Try easier Bell Rock Loops first. Bell Rock Path is the "launch ramp" to single track on both sides of HWY 179. Llama connects Submarine Rock Loop and Bell Rock/Courthouse Loops bypassing the urban trail. Shred Submarine Rock Loop then tunnel under HWY 179 via Templeton Trail to Cathedral Rock Loop and Buddha Beach. See the map.

SEDONA

# SECRET TRAILS

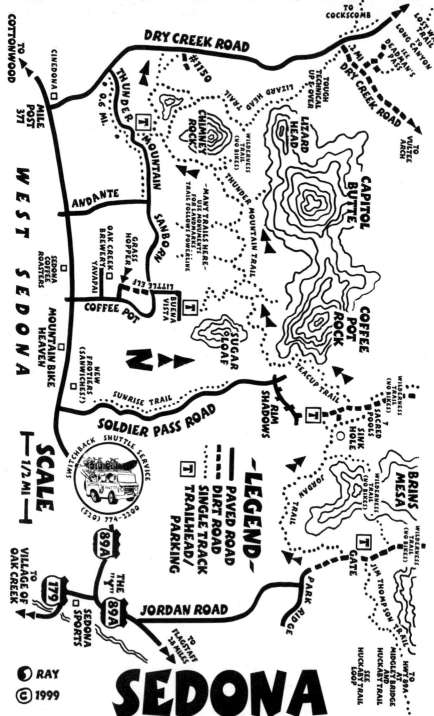

SEDONA

© RAY
Ⓒ 1999

# *Sedona* **SECRET TRAILS**
## WAY FUN HIDDEN SINGLE TRACK

**DISTANCE:** 10 PLUS MILES
**TIME:** 2 to 3 HOURS
**EFFORT:** TOUGH
**SKILL:** ADVANCED
**PUCK-O-METER:** PUCK 8
SOME EXPOSURE AND BIG DROPS
**ROUTE:** MOSTLY SIGNED
**SEASON:** SEP to JUN

**AT A GLANCE**

5000

**ELEV. (FT.)**

4500

O     **MILES**     10

**DESCRIPTION:** Secret no mo'! A helter-skelter welter of single-track is linked, signed and cairned to connect a short cut across Sedona from Schnebly Hill Rd. to Dry Creek Rd.

    From Schnebly Hill, Huckaby Trail hugs a cliff then dives down across Oak Creek and back up to 89A at Midgley Bridge. Connect with Jim Thompson Trail to climb up and over Uptown Sedona. See "Huckaby Trail" for map details.

    Jordan (formerly "Secret") Trail roller coasters along the base of Brin's Mesa then flushes you out at the sinkhole in Devils Kitchen where you find signs to Teacup Trail. If you crave exposure to ledge death risk, this will be just your cup of tea. Later, up on top, you spy a power line and follow it to Chimney Rock as you hit Thunder Mountain Trail which dumps you out on Dry Creek Road. Pick up Lost Watch Trail (unsigned, see map) and head to Long Canyon for Deadman's Pass Trail (see "Deadman's Pass") and Cockscomb Loop.

    Many trails are signed and often marked with industrial size cairns, but not always. Look up! Enjoy the view. Stay un-lost Sedona style. Eyeball big red rocks like Capitol, Coffee Pot and Chimney to keep your bearings.

*"All who wander are not lost."*
*J.R.R. Tolkien*

**SEDONA**

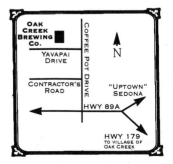

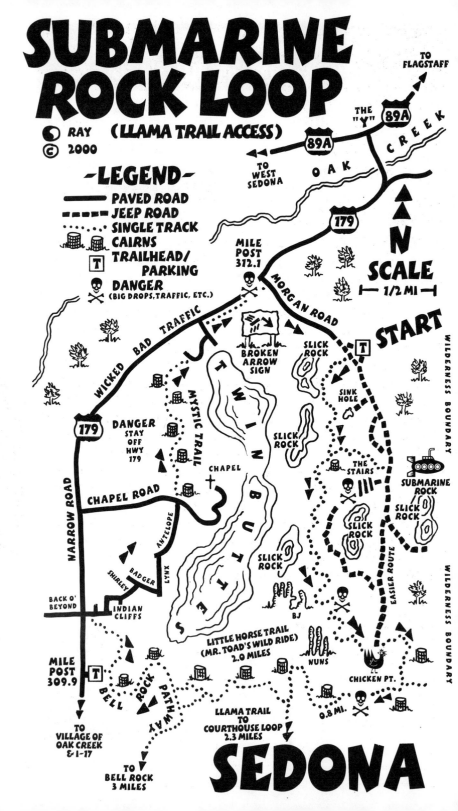

# SUBMARINE ROCK LOOP
## SEDONA'S PREMIER SHRED

**DISTANCE:** 10 MILE LOOP
**TIME:** 2 to 3 HOURS
**EFFORT:** HARD WORK
**SKILL:** EXPERT
**PUCK-O-METER:** PUCK 9
SPEED, BIG DROPS AND "THE STAIRS"
**FIND ROUTE:** MODERATE
**SEASON:** SEP to MAY

**AT A GLANCE**

4500

**ELEV. (FT.)**

4000

O    **LOOP MILES**    10

**DESCRIPTION:** The most bang for your biking buck. Slickrock, single track, stairs and even a Mr. Toad's wild ride. If you've got time for just one Sedona ride, this is it.

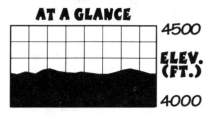

**PRIMO TRAIL**

The basic loop begins with a rough jeep road at the end of Morgan Road. See the map. Across the road from the parking area is a well marked, way fun single track following a higher and tougher route to Chicken Point. Be sure to visit the sinkhole, The Stairs, and of course, Subrock.

Eventually you wind up at Chicken Point. From Chicken, back up 50 feet and you'll find the hidden single track down to Little Horse Trail. This 2 mile stretch is called Mr. Toad's Wild Ride and is well marked with giant bomber cairns. Watch out for steep drops as this little beauty screams and careens downhill almost all the way.

**OPTIONS:** 0.8 miles after you leave Chicken Point, unmarked but well worn and legal Llama Trail veers off toward Courthouse Rock. You can continue and follow the map to finish the *Subrock Loop* or go LEFT to *Courthouse Loop Trail* and connect with *Cathedral Rock Loop.* (Lookit da' Llama Trail map!)

**DIRECTIONS:** DON'T RIDE HWY 179. It's deadly. *DRIVE* to the Morgan Road start. Morgan Road is easy to find on HWY 179 at milepost 312.1. A "Broken Arrow" sign marks the turn. If the Morgan Road lot is full, park and start at Little Horse trailhead at milepost 309.9.

*"Don't take life seriously or you won't get out alive, Doc."*
*-Bugs Bunny*

**SEDONA**

# 50 YEAR TRAIL
## (THE CHUTES)

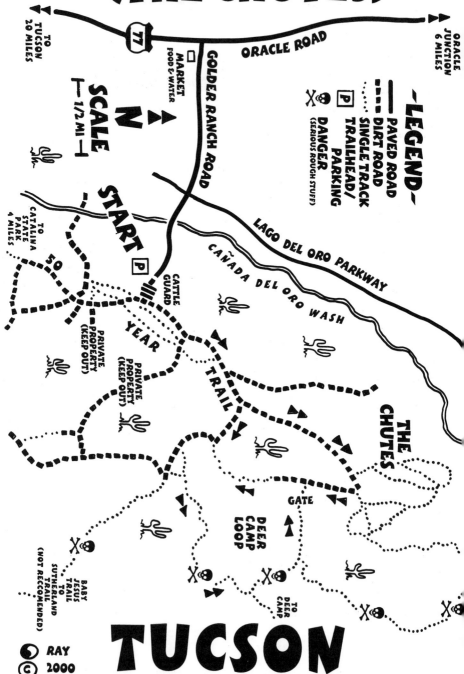

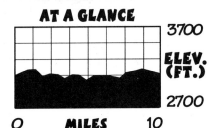

# Tucson **50 YEAR TRAIL**
## EXCELLENT CHUTES & SINGLE TRACK

**DISTANCE:** 10 MILES PLUS
**TIME:** 2 TO 3 HOURS
**EFFORT:** A GOOD SWEAT
**SKILL:** INTERMEDIATE TO
    ADVANCED
**PUCK-O-METER:** PUCK 7
SPEED THRU TECHNICAL SECTIONS
**FIND ROUTE:** MODERATE
**SEASON:** SEP to JUN

**AT A GLANCE**

3700

ELEV.
(FT.)

2700

0     **MILES**     10

**DESCRIPTION:** Rolling single track horse trails and jeep roads run amuck all over this prime Sonoran Desert in the western foothills of the Santa Catalina Mountains just north of Tucson. The trails climb, rip, jump, twist and plunge through a scatter of saguaro standing amid the lush desert vegetation. You can't get too lost as The Catalinas loom overhead making for great scenic landmarks.

I like it best in the cooler months when everything is green and creeks are running, but good all year except in the full on dead heat of a summer day. Ride early then.

You'll twist up some good loops from the map. Near the mountains to the east, the terrain gets tougher and rougher. And DO NOT MISS THE CHUTES! They are a way bitchin' cactus lined roller coaster of twisty, turny horse and motorcycle worn trails that will make you shout.

**DIRECTIONS:** Head due north out of Tucson on State Highway Route 77 (Oracle Road) toward Oracle Junction. It's about 20miles to the Golder Ranch Road turn. There is a mini-mart on the corner to load up on pop-tarts (just kidding!) before you hit the trail. Go to the end of Golder Ranch to where it turns dirt. Park in the lot. Get on your bike, cross the cattleguard and get on the singletrack heading north. Follow "50 YEAR TRAIL" signs, consult the map from time to time and not to worry about getting lost. The Catalinas are always overhead to the east.

**TUCSON**

# BUTTERFLY TRAIL
## (F-86 FIGHTER CRASH SITE)

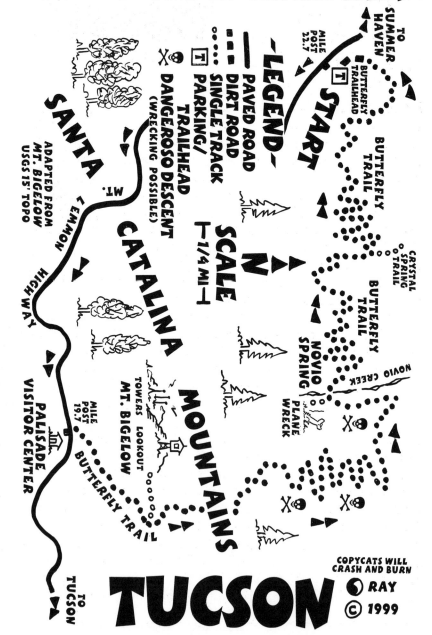

TUCSON

COPYCATS WILL CRASH AND BURN

RAY

© 1999

# Tucson BUTTERFLY TRAIL LOOP
## GREAT SINGLE TRACK TO JET WRECK

**DISTANCE:** 9 MILE LOOP
**TIME:** 2 to 3 HOURS
**EFFORT:** HARD WORK
**SKILL:** EXPERT
**PUCK-O-METER:** PUCK 9
STEEP DESCENT WITH BIG DROPS
**FIND ROUTE:** EASY
**SEASON:** MAR to DEC

**AT A GLANCE**

9000
ELEV.
(FT.)
6500

O  **LOOP MILES**  9.0

**DESCRIPTION:** *Summer!* Your tires could *melt* in Tucson. Get up to 8200' on Mt. Lemmon and catch a chill. Descend a way cool, twisty, technical single track with loads of hairy exposure through conifer, aspen and oak. View superb reds and golds in fall. You'll need nerve and a monster fat rig to match.

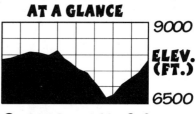

Check out the cool F-86 Sabrejet that augered in 1955. Big chunks still about plus lots of smaller bits. The pilot bailed and lived. This badass fighter bomber carried six .50 cal machine guns, a ton of bombs and sixteen 5' rockets. F-86s killed 792 MIG-15s over Korea while losing only 76 of their own. A 10 to 1 kill ratio! Its solo turbine produced 6000 pounds of thrust. Now that's what I call urge. Sure wish I could get my hands on just one of those 5' rockets. Yeah baby!

## MILEAGE LOG

0.0 Avoid needless anguish. DO THIS LOOP COUNTER-CLOCKWISE. START at Butterfly Trailhead at Mile 22.7 on Mt. Lemmon Highway. Ride pavement back up to Palisade Visitor Center at Mile 19.7.

3.0 Head up trail directly across from Palisade Visitor Center toward Mt. Bigelow Lookout.

3.6 Junction to Mt. Bigelow Lookout. Continue on Butterfly Trail and begin severe 1440' descent.

6.0 Novio Spring. Before you cross this intermittent creek, take the trail above and along the stream a few hundred feet to the F-86 stackage. Worth it. Now start the relentless UP back to the trailhead.

9.0 Butterfly Trailhead back where you began. Proceed to Summerhaven for a most excellent homemade pie fest at Mt. Lemmon Cafe. Yum!

**TUCSON**

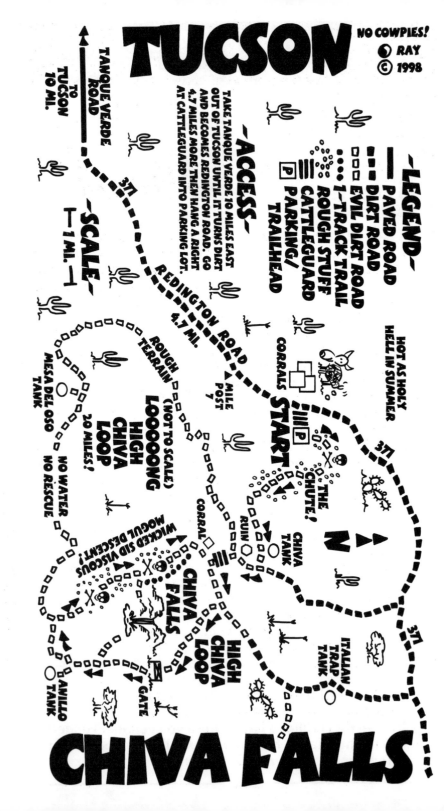

# *Tucson* CHIVA FALLS
## TOUGH 2-TRACK TO A BRIDAL VEIL

**DISTANCE:** 8.4 MILES
**TIME:** 3 HOURS
**EFFORT:** TOUGH
**SKILL:** EXPERT
**PUCK-O-METER:** PUCK 9
RAPID JACKHAMMER DESCENTS
**FIND ROUTE:** MODERATE
**SEASON:** SEP to MAY

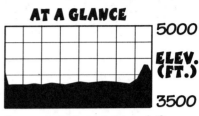

**AT A GLANCE**

5000

**ELEV. (FT.)**

3500

0   **1-WAY MILES**   4.2

**DESCRIPTION:** Chiva runs late fall to spring. Perfect spot to dip your buns on a hot day. The falls cascade 60ft. to a pool 3ft. deep and 50 ft. wide set in a verdant stone grotto. The Rincons are overhead south. There is a simple out n' back, a favorite high loop above the falls or a veeery long version. All are rough 2-track with double skull Sid Viscous descents. Carry water and munchies.

### OUT AND BACK TO CHIVA

0.0 START (see map) east end of parking lot and head down the ultra rough 2-track.
2.6 RIGHT at "T" junction just past Chiva Tank.
3.4 Veer LEFT over cattleguard.
3.5 RIGHT at junction.
3.7 Wash crossings then a single track heading up.
4.0 LEFT at fork. Continue 0.2 miles to the falls.
8.4 Return to GO all shook up!

### HIGH CHIVA LOOP

**DESCRIPTION:** Best loop in the Rincons. Same start as out n' back, but after cattleguard turn LEFT at next junction. 0.4 miles later a faint 2-track heads uphill to the RIGHT. 1.8 miles later cross Chiva Creek above the falls. Great for exploring, lots of pools and a good spot for lunch. A mile after you leave Chiva Creek make a RIGHT at a

PRIMO

TRAIL

junction that takes you down ☠heinous descent☠ to Chiva. It's a 12 mile total loop. **TOUGH OPTION:** If you go LEFT at that same junction you are on the Long High Loop. Make sure you have plenty of food, water and daylight. It's a looong 20 mile loop even for fit expert riders.

TUCSON

# CRYSTAL SPRING TRAIL

ADAPTED FROM
**MT. BIGELOW**
AND
**MT. LEMMON**
USGS 15' TOPOS

MT. LEMMON CONTROL ROAD — FS 38

UP UP UP

**N**

SCALE
1/2 MI

TO SUMMER HAVEN

MT. LEMMON HIGHWAY

SANTA

CRYSTAL

CATALINA

SPRING

MOUNTAINS

CRYSTAL SPRING

TRAIL

**START**

BUTTERFLY PEAK

BUTTERFLY TRAIL

MILE POST 22.7

T

BUTTERFLY TRAILHEAD

SEE "BUTTERFLY TRAIL"

## —LEGEND—

— **PAVED ROAD**
▬▬▬ **ROUGH DIRT ROAD**
○○○○ **SINGLE TRACK**
T **PARKING/ TRAILHEAD**
☠ **DANGER (STEEP)**

TO TUCSON

◑ RAY
© 1999

# TUCSON

# Tucson CRYSTAL SPRING TRAIL
## SINGLE TRACK LOOP HIGH ON MT. LEMMON

**DISTANCE:** 10 MILES
**TIME:** 2 to 4 HOURS
**EFFORT:** FAIRLY HARD
**SKILL:** ADVANCED
**PUCK-O-METER:** PUCK 7.5
HIGH SPEED NARROW DESCENT
**FIND ROUTE:** EASY
**SEASON:** MAR to NOV

AT A GLANCE
8000
ELEV. (FT.)
6000
O   LOOP MILES   10

**DESCRIPTION:** Great way to get out of the broiler and onto nearby cool forest trails when Tucson temps hit triple digits. Enjoy views from the top of Mt. Lemmon. Fly down a wicked single track and climb back a rough scenic jeep road. Finish on a short paved bit to your transpo.

### MILEAGE LOG

0.0  START at Butterfly Trailhead at Milepost 22.7 on the Mt. Lemmon (Catalina) Highway. Butterfly Trail is signed and takes off behind the gate at the north end north end of the parking lot. Stay left and the trail quickly turns into a rapid and twisting single track descent. Watch for hikers on this first bit.

1.2  Butterfly meets with Crystal Spring Trail. Trail junction is signed. Go LEFT and continue down toward Crystal Spring. Lots of views, exposure and way fun twisty-turny single track as the trail heads down and across the northeast face of the mountain past Crystal Spring through a mixed forest of conifer, oak and aspen. Finally, Crystal Spring Trail steeply corkscrews down a serious set of switchbacks and connects with Mt. Lemmon Control Road.

5.0  LEFT on Mt. Lemmon Control Road and crank up the 1200', 3 mile jeep road climb back to pavement where you again meet Mt. Lemmon Highway.

8.0  Whew! What a grunt. You top out at paved Mt. Lemmon Highway. Go LEFT back to Butterfly Trailhead OR hang a right for a short detour and hit Summerhaven for some great eats at Mt. Lemmon Cafe. Their home made pies be the best in the west.

10.0 Back to Butterfly Trailhead. Hope you did the pie and coffee thing. I mean what's the point of all this work if you can't enjoy a little apres shred snackage.

TUCSON

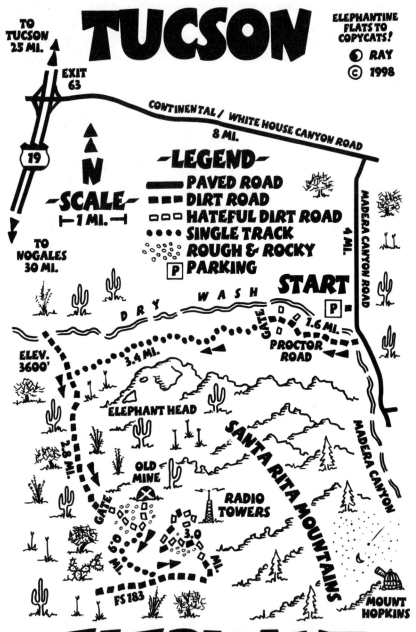

# TUCSON

ELEPHANTINE FLATS TO COPYCATS!

🌓 RAY
© 1998

TO TUCSON 25 MI.

EXIT 63

CONTINENTAL / WHITE HOUSE CANYON ROAD

8 MI.

19

N

4 MI.

MADERA CANYON ROAD

## LEGEND

—— PAVED ROAD
- - - DIRT ROAD
▢▢▢ HATEFUL DIRT ROAD
•••• SINGLE TRACK
⊙ ROUGH & ROCKY
P PARKING

SCALE
1 MI.

TO NOGALES 30 MI.

DRY WASH

START

P

GATE

1.6 MI.

PROCTOR ROAD

ELEV. 3600'

3.4 MI.

ELEPHANT HEAD

2.8 MI.

GATE

OLD MINE

RADIO TOWERS

SANTA RITA MOUNTAINS

MADERA CANYON

.60 MI.

3.0 MI.

FS 183

MOUNT HOPKINS

# ELEPHANT HEAD
# (SANTA RITA MOUNTAINS)

# Tucson ELEPHANT HEAD
## GREAT TRAIL IN THE SANTA RITAS

**DISTANCE:** 24 MILES
**TIME:** 3 to 5 HOURS
**EFFORT:** TOUGH
**SKILL:** INTERMEDIATE
**PUCK-O-METER:** PUCK 7.5
FAST DESCENTS ON RETURN TRIP
**FIND ROUTE:** MODERATE
**SEASON:** SEP to MAY

**AT A GLANCE**

6000
ELEV.
(FT.)
3500

O **1-WAY MILES** 12

**DESCRIPTION:** Excellent single track and scenery in the Santa Ritas south of Tucson. Color and shadows play across broken granite creating illusions for your viewing pleasure. Save this ride for the cooler months when streams are running and the giant saguaro sonoran desert is lush with life and full of birdsong.

South from Tucson 25 miles on I-19, take the Continental exit and head east 12 miles on Madera Canyon Road. Proctor Road is well marked. Proctor soon goes all to hell and turns single track through the ocotillo, saguaro and mesquite. Frequent stream crossings in the wet months. Finally there's a humongo climb to the radio towers. The trail is well marked. Bring lots of water and a snack. I got so hungry I nearly ate my shoe. Yum!

## MILEAGE LOG

0.0 PARK in the lot. Follow Proctor Rd. gradually downhill. Keep a sharp eye out for bike trail signs.
1.6 Through a wash then a gate. Great single track.
5.0 Another gate, then a dirt road. Go LEFT. Begin climb.
7.8 Short steep single track heads up to the RIGHT off the jeep road before the old mine. Not obvious. Keep your eyes peeled for the trail sign.
8.0 A little pass. Check the view then CONTINUE.
8.7 LEFT on F.S. 183 right after a stream crossing. Head up to the towers.
12.0 Towers. View. The whole enchilada. Enjoy the descent.
24.0 Return to the start.

"To be on one's bike is the ultimate goal of all ambition."
- mountain bike wisdom

**TUCSON**

BROADWAY

TO DOWNTOWN TUCSON 8 MILES

HARRISON 2 MILES

START

HOUGHTON

PERMIT INFO
TUCSON AREA
STATE TRUST LAND
(520) 628-5480

IRVINGTON

T

ONE WAY

ONE WAY

N
~SCALE~
1/4 MI

JUMP OR DIE

ONE WAY

STATE TRUST LAND

HALF PIPE

NEW KILLER SINGLE TRACK LOOP

ONE WAY

ONE WAY

ONE WAY

MAIN LOOP

ONE WAY

~LEGEND~
———— PAVED STREET
········· SINGLE TRACK
T TRAILHEAD/ PARKING
☠ DANGER
(BIG DROP, DEEP WASH, BIG LEAP, ETC.)

BONUS LOOP

ONE WAY

ONE WAY

ONE WAY

ONE WAY

*FANTASY ISLAND*

TUCSON

⊙ RAY
© 2001
DEATH TO COPYCAT

# Tucson FANTASY ISLAND LOOPS
## SINGLE TRACK, DEATH LEAP & A HALF PIPE

**DISTANCE:** 10 MILES
**TIME:** 2 TO ??? HOURS
**EFFORT:** EASY, BUT...
(GO FASTER, WORK HARDER, DO IT TWICE!)
**SKILL:** ALL LEVELS
**PUCK-O-METER:** PUCK 6
(SOME PUCK 10 STUFF TOO!)
**FIND ROUTE:** SIGNED
(FOLLOW THE ONE WAY LOOPS)
**SEASON:** SEP TO MAY

**AT A GLANCE**

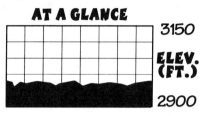

3150

**ELEV.
(FT.)**

2900

O   **LOOP MILES**   10

**DESCRIPTION:** Picture pee-wee golf, chutes & ladders, single track, big drops, a do-or-die death jump and a rock 'n roll half-pipe. There is no destination on this trail. The destination IS the trail. The best desert flat track you will ever ride. Perfect for all levels. Speed as fast as you dare through the half pipe. Look out for

**PRIMO**

**TRAIL**

big drops. The trail is a well marked, worn in, winding snake loop that never crosses itself. Ideal for single speeds, no big climbs, tight and twisty, all right turns. You will not get lost. COUNTER-CLOCKWISE ONLY.

This is an ingenious bit of master trail building art making the most of a small pristine plot of giant saguaro sonoran desert. Fantasy Island Loop is on a less than 2 square mile hunk of State Trust Land. The basic loop has a half-pipe, lotsa twisties and some big drops. Out on the extra new bonus loops you're gonna find more of the same with one great jump-or-die heart stopper.

Support cooperation between the State Land Dept. and the Tucson mountain bike community. Permits are $15/year, good on any trust land in AZ. Get them from the state land office, 223 N. Main, Tucson (520-628-5480) or at Broadway Bicycles, Lone Cactus Bicycles or Sabino Bicycles. Worth every penny.

**DIRECTIONS:** From downtown Tucson go 8 miles east on Broadway to Harrison Road. Turn RIGHT on Harrison then go another 2 miles to Irvington and park at the gate.

"Life is a daring adventure or nothing at all."
- mountain bike wisdom

**TUCSON**

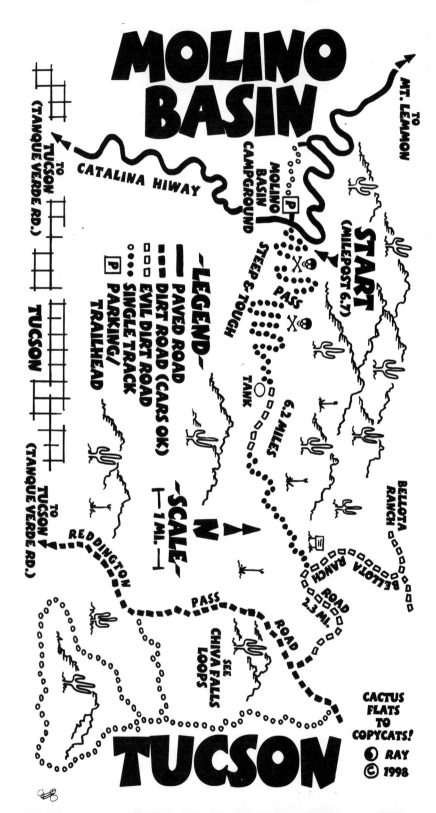

# *Tucson* **MOLINO BASIN**
## GREAT SINGLE TRACK OUT AND BACK

**DISTANCE:** 12.4 MILES
**TIME:** 3 to 4 HOURS
**EFFORT:** TOUGH
**SKILL:** ADVANCED
**PUCK-O-METER:** PUCK 6.5
  STEEP TWISTING DESCENT
**FIND ROUTE:** EASY
**SEASON:** OCT to MAY

**AT A GLANCE**

5000

**ELEV. (FT.)**

4000

O  **1-WAY MILES**  6.2

**DESCRIPTION:** Starts out as a way steep single track leads up over a pass out of Molino Basin followed by a monster steep technical single track down the other side. Feels like a lifetime, but it's only been 2 miles, under and hour and the best is yet to come. Next, a quick rolling 1-track leads you another 4 miles all the way to Bellota Ranch Road where you turn about and return.

## MILEAGE LOG

**0.0** START at Molino Basin Campground parking lot at mile 6.7 on Catalina Hiway heading up Mt. Lemmon out of Tucson. The steep technical 1-track climb begins through a row of boulders across the road.

**0.9** SUMMIT. Views into Molino Basin and out to the Rincons. HEAD DOWN other side to West Spring.

**2.1** WEST SPRING. You came this far, might as well go on for a great 1-track to Bellota Ranch Road.

**6.2** BELLOTA RANCH RD. Good spot to turn n' burn OR continue RIGHT 2.3 miles to Reddington Road and meet a support for a 1-way ride. Bellota Ranch meets Reddington on left at mile 7.4 on Reddington.

**12.4** Back to GO. if you rode the pass twice, I'm with you. We don't need no stinking cars!

**OPTIONS:** Employ a shuttle on Reddington Road and make this a moderate 1-way ride OR maybe START at the other end on Reddington for just the easy 1-track. Thank explorer Jim Porter for his pioneer work on Molino Basin.

> "It ain't the 'untin' as 'urts 'im.
> It's the 'ammer, 'ammer, 'ammer on the 'ard 'igh road."
> - *Punch, 1856 ( quote thanks to Jim Porter)*

**TUCSON**

# PEPPERSAUCE LOOP

℗ RAY
© 1998

NO COPIES POLEEZ!

-LEGEND-

- - - GRADED DIRT ROAD
□ □ PRIMITIVE ROAD
× × ROUGH, ROCKY & HEINOUS
〜 INTERMITTENT STREAM
P PARKING/TRAILHEAD

GREAT VIEWS

0.5 MI.

0.1

JACKHAMMER HILL (ROCKY STEEP DESCENT) 2.2 MI.

EASY UP

CORONADO

MORE EVIL UP

NATIONAL

EVIL CLIMB

5.9 MI.

ABANDONED MINE

FOREST

PEPPERSAUCE CREEK (FAST & FUN)

FS 29

PEPPERSAUCE CAMPGROUND

P

START

FS 38

TO ORACLE 8 MI. TUCSON 43 MI.

MOUNT

EASY UP

EASY LEMMON

2.6 MI.

-SCALE-
1/2 MI.

N

PEPPERSAUCE CAVE

LEMMON ROAD FS 38

EASY UP

YE OLDE BRIDGE

FS 38

TO THE TOP OF MT. LEMMON

# TUCSON
# (ORACLE)

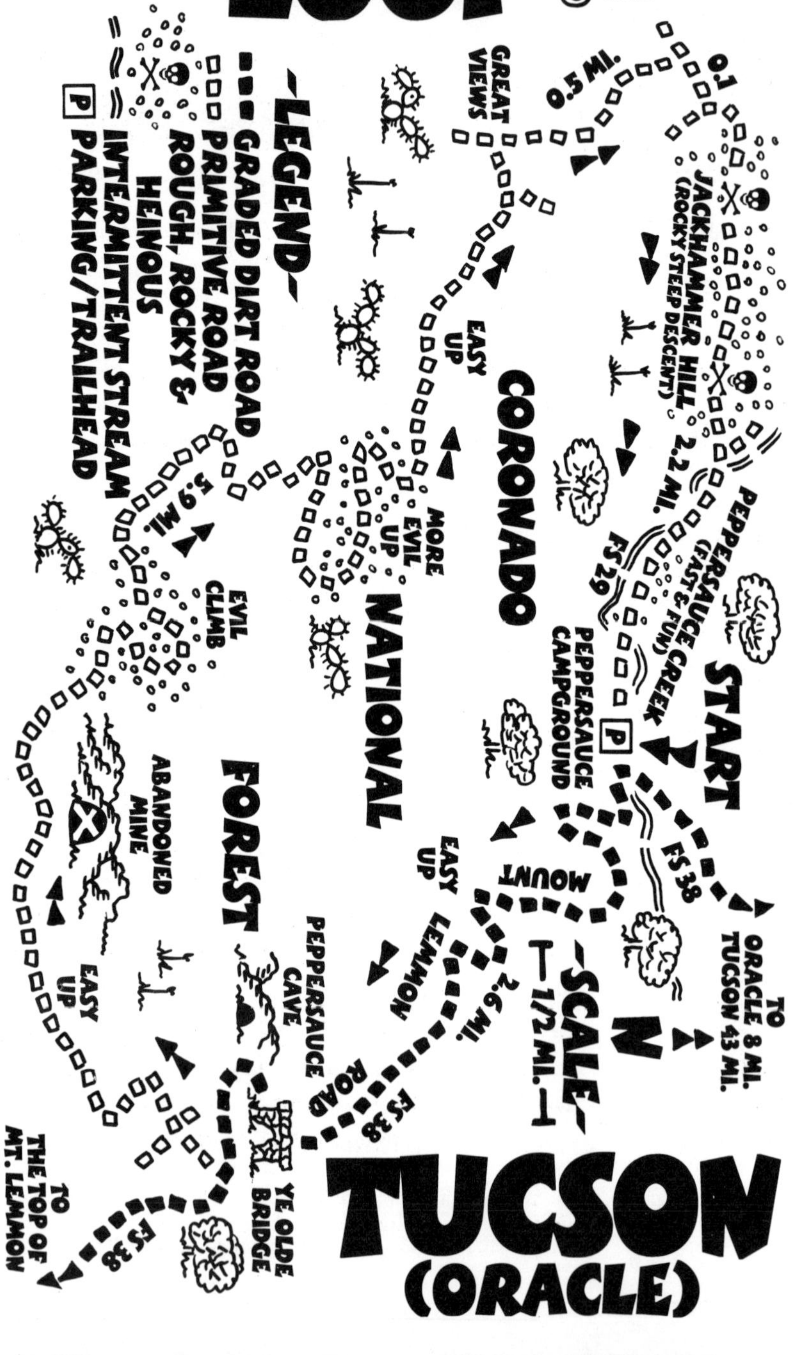

# Tucson PEPPERSAUCE LOOP
## TOUGH JEEP ROAD LOOP TO VIEWS

**DISTANCE:** 11 MILES
**TIME:** 3 to 4 HOURS
**EFFORT:** SEVERE
**SKILL:** EXPERTO
**PUCK-O-METER:** PUCK 8.5
HIGH SPEED JACKHAMMER DESCENT
**FIND ROUTE:** MODERATE
**SEASON:** OCT to MAY

**AT A GLANCE**

7000

**ELEV. (FT.)**

4500

O **LOOP MILES** 11

**DESCRIPTION:** This wicked buttruff runs all over the hills above Oracle along rugged Oracle Ridge. It's tough bumpy fun. In the spring when creeks are running you might even get wet. Not a ride for the dead of summer when it's drier than a popcorn fart unless you start at zero-dark-thirty. Pack plenty of water and snacks.

      Peppersauce is 45 miles north of Tucson and 8 miles out of Oracle. Head out Mount Lemmon Control Road. The pavement ends and turns to dirt. Park at Peppersauce Campground. Strap a pillow to your seat for the double skull evil Jackhammer Hill descent and GO!

### MILEAGE LOG

0.0 From campground, CONTINUE up Mt.Lemmon Road.

2.6 RIGHT turn uphill onto a rough jeep road.

2.8 CONTINUE STRAIGHT downhill from a crossroads. Next 5.7 miles stay on this road. After passing old mine the rough climb begins. The next two miles take you up and up. At the top check out a view of the Galiuro Mountains to the north then tackle the steep rollers coming up.

8.5 CONTINUE past spur on the right and a small pond.

8.6 RIGHT at "T" junction.

9.1 Bear RIGHT at fork and down (OUCH!) Jackhammer Hill. You have to be mental to enjoy this stuff.

9.7 Whew! Jackhammer stops and you continue to follow Peppersauce Canyon swooping back down. Yes!

11.3 There you are. The end. Hope you brought a frosty.

*"Youth, strength and ambition always may be overcome by memory, experience and treachery."*
*- I forget which old fart said that.*

**TUCSON**

# SAGUARO NATIONAL MONUMENT EAST

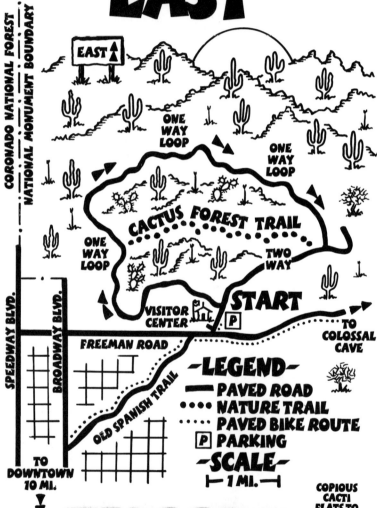

EAST

CORONADO NATIONAL FOREST

NATIONAL MONUMENT BOUNDARY

ONE WAY LOOP

ONE WAY LOOP

ONE WAY LOOP

CACTUS FOREST TRAIL

TWO WAY

VISITOR CENTER

START

P

TO COLOSSAL CAVE

SPEEDWAY BLVD.

BROADWAY BLVD.

FREEMAN ROAD

OLD SPANISH TRAIL

~LEGEND~
— PAVED ROAD
•••• NATURE TRAIL
•••• PAVED BIKE ROUTE
P PARKING

~SCALE~
⊢ 1 MI. ⊣

TO DOWNTOWN 10 MI.

# TUCSON

COPIOUS CACTI FLATS TO COPYCATS!

☾ RAY
© 1998

# Tucson GIANT SAGUARO EAST
## CACTUS FOREST TRAIL LOOP

**DISTANCE:** 7 MILES
**TIME:** 2 HOURS
**EFFORT:** FAIRLY EASY
**SKILL:** NOVICE
**PUCK-O-METER:** PUCK 2
NO PANIC, BUT STAY ON TRAIL
**FIND ROUTE:** EASY
**SEASON:** SEP to MAY

**AT A GLANCE**

2700

**ELEV. (FT.)**

2200

O   **LOOP MILES**   7

**DESCRIPTION:** Easy rolling Cactus Forest Trail in Saguaro Monument East is a stroll in a botanical garden. Beautiful, wild and you don't even have to leave the city.

Giant saguaro represent the southwest. Our logo so to speak. They inspire amusement when they don a technicolor hat of flowers and look as though they're about to dance. Saguaro grow to a height of 50 ft. and weigh up to 8 tons as they live out their 150 years, yet begin as a seed no larger than the period at the end of this sentence. A saguaro may produce 40 million seeds, yet only one will survive. A year to grow it's 1st quarter inch, a foot in 15 years and 75 years to sprout arms. The saguaro is monarch of an alien world with summer temps over 115°. These guys can drink 200 gallons of water in one gulp and make it last a year. Wow!

All life here, including the good people of Tucson, has adapted to survive a hostile environment making for a wonderfully diverse and beautiful set of creatures. The saguaro is home to owls, hawks, woodpeckers, wrens, sparrows and martins who live in its tiny apartments. Nearby you find javelina, rattlers, gila monsters, tortoises, rabbits, quail, mice and on and on. Flowers, trees, shrubs and cacti of every size and shape fill out the picture. Who says the desert is a barren place?

This is a national monument run by the park service. It will cost you a couple of bucks to enter. The trail is a one-way that bisects the park's paved loop road. BEGIN on the paved road to the RIGHT as you enter (less pavement to the trailhead). Stay on the trail. Carry plenty of water and a snack. Makes for a great family outing.

**TUCSON**

# Tucson SAMANIEGO RIDGE
## MONSTER SINGLE TRACK DESCENT

**DISTANCE:** 21 MILES
**TIME:** 6 HOURS
**EFFORT:** LONG HARD RIDE
**SKILL:** ADVANCED
**PUCK-O-METER:** PUCK 10
STEEP, BRAIDED CHAROULEAU DESCENT
**FIND ROUTE:** MODERATE
**SEASON:** APR to OCT

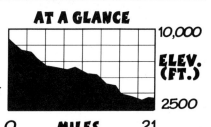

AT A GLANCE

10,000

**ELEV.
(FT.)**

2500

O          MILES          21

**DESCRIPTION:** My mental image of Burly Bubbas and Buff Bettys flying down no rescue Samaniego Ridge at warp speed scares the heck outa me, so I tell this tale with fair warning. We three had five good diggers. You may end up on the evening news. However, though leaking the sicky sweet smell of fear (beer?) from every pore, we did do it and lived. What the hey, no brain no gain!

OK, that said, kiss the family good bye. The 6000 ft. drop begins top of Mt. Lemmon behind the power station at the end of Ski Run Rd. Find it on the map. The Sutherland Trail 1-track runs quickly down 2 miles to the Samaniego Ridge Trail junction. Go RIGHT and stay on rough rolling, but generally downhill Samaniego Ridge for 7.8 miles *down to the TOP* of Charouleau Gap. I say *generally* down cuz there are lots of ups and downs through real abusive terrain. Careful not to turf it. You're in sight of Tucson, but rescue here could take time. Be advised!

Top of Charouleau Gap. By this time we had been on the trail for hours and had stacked many times already. We were tired and not ready to roll the heinous hairball descent. Charouleau is way steep, slippery, bumpy, braided hardpack jeep road. More mechanical carnage. 5 riding and wrecking miles later the trail dumps into the Canada del Oro dry wash. Anyway, you better hope it's dry. At times, Canada del Oro gets way big and uncrossable.

It's a long hilly paved 5 mile crawl to the convenience store on the corner of Golder Ranch and Oracle Rd. where the support ambulance is hopefully waiting. Glug a dewey brew and there you are . . . body and bike broken, brain bent and your spirit free as a bird!

**TUCSON**

# TUCSON MNTS

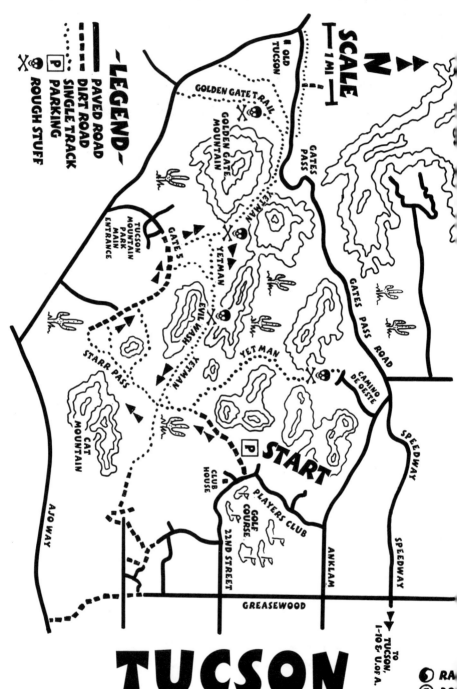

N

## SCALE
1 MI

## —LEGEND—
- PAVED ROAD
- DIRT ROAD
- SINGLE TRACK
- P PARKING
- ROUGH STUFF

OLD TUCSON

GOLDEN GATE TRAIL

GOLDEN GATE MOUNTAIN

GATES PASS

YETMAN

TUCSON MOUNTAIN PARK MAIN ENTRANCE

GATE 5

YETMAN

EVIL WASH

YETMAN

GATES PASS ROAD

STARR PASS

YETMAN

YETMAN

CAMINO DE OESTE

CAT MOUNTAIN

SPEEDWAY

START

P

CLUB HOUSE

PLAYERS CLUB

GOLF COURSE

AJO WAY

22ND STREET

ANKLAM

SPEEDWAY

GREASEWOOD

TO TUCSON, I-10 &, U. OF A.

# TUCSON

RA
© 20

**DISTANCE:** 7.7 MILE LOOP
**TIME:** 2 HOURS
**EFFORT:** MODERATE
**SKILL:** MODERATE
**PUCK-O-METER:** PUCK 7
SOME ROUGH STUFF, BUT NOT BAD
**FIND ROUTE:** MODERATE
**SEASON:** SEP to JUN

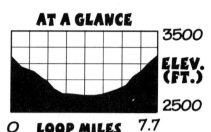

**AT A GLANCE**

3500

**ELEV. (FT.)**

2500

O    **LOOP MILES**    7.7

**DESCRIPTION:** *The* classic Tucson shred. Fast, intermediate desert single track with a little rough stuff. Giant saguaro forest. Great expansive views. Plenty of wildlife, especially coyote and javelina early mornings. Close to town and easy to find.

### MILEAGE LOG

0.0 Park in the lot. Step over the gate. Go 50 yards to the sign marked "Starr Pass". Go LEFT and follow the power lines over Starr Pass.

1.5 Step over gate. Turn RIGHT and continue on 1-track along the park boundary until it becomes a dirt road then look for faintly marked Gate 5 on your right.

3.3 RIGHT on through Gate 5 to Yetman Trail junction. Look around. A left takes you up to Gates Pass.

4.7 RIGHT onto Yetman Trail, so rough it'll knock the plaque off your teeth and save you a trip to the dentist. Yetman leads into a wash . Fist to brain size boulders knock you around pretty good.

6.7 Back to the Starr Pass Trail junction. Go LEFT and follow the power lines back up to where you parked.

7.7 Back to GO. Check out some other great trails in the Tucson Mountains. Good exploring here.

**DIRECTIONS:** Follow the map. Head west out notorious and aptly named main drag Speedway. If you can't find Speedway, you are indeed lost! Go under the freeway. LEFT on Greasewood. RIGHT on Anklam. LEFT on unmarked Players Club at the "STARR PASS" sign. LEFT at "T" intersection then take first RIGHT. Probably still not paved. Park where the road ends.

"A starry night can quiet the soul."
-Vincent Van Go

**TUCSON**

# THUMPER TRAIL LOOP
## (DEAD HORSE PARK)

**-LEGEND-**
- ──────── PAVED ROAD
- ▪▪▪▪ ROUGH 2-TRACK
- •••• SINGLE TRACK
- P PARKING
- T TRAILHEAD
- THUMPER TRAIL CAIRN

STEEP ROUGH DESCENT TO PECKS LAKE & TUZIGOOT 2.5 MILES

BONES TRAIL

ELEV. 3900'

RAPTOR HILL TRAIL

THUMPER TRAIL

GATE

N
SCALE
⊢ 1/2 MI. ⊣

UP

DOWN

THUMPER LOOP

BEST BET IS TO PARK AT THE BALLFIELDS FOR FREE AND RIDE INTO THE STATE PARK.

STEEP UP

ELEV. 3200'

GATE

UP

**START** T **GATE**

**STAY ON TRAIL**
ENDANGERED PLANT SPECIES
(ARIZONA CLIFF ROSE)

DOWN

LIME KILN TRAIL

PARK ENTRANCE

CAMP
CAMP
CAMP
DAY USE

FISHING LAGOON

DOWN

◐ RAY
© 1999
NO COPIES PLEASE!

BRIDGE

TO CLARKDALE

BALL FIELDS P VERDE RIVER

N. 10TH ST.
S. MAIN ST.

TO HWY 89A SEDONA & FLAGSTAFF

| DEAD HORSE STATE PARK | |
|---|---|
| BIKE | $1 |
| CAR | $4 |
| CAMPING | $10 |
| W/HOOK-UP | $15 |

THANKS TO
KARL & ALLYSON
MINGUS MOUNTAIN BIKES
203 S. MAIN
COTTONWOOD

# COTTONWOOD

# Cottonwood THUMPER LOOP
## FUN SINGLE TRACK LOOP ON THE VERDE

**DISTANCE:** 8 MILE LOOP
**TIME:** 0.5 to 1.5 HOURS
**EFFORT:** SOME SWEAT
**SKILL:** INTERMEDIATE
**PUCK-O-METER:** PUCK 7.5
A FEW TECH BITS ON THE DESCENT
**FIND ROUTE:** EASY
**SEASON:** OCT to MAY

**AT A GLANCE**

4500

**ELEV. (FT.)**

3000

O    **LOOP MILES**    8

**DESCRIPTION:** Thumper is a fine short loop anytime, but an especially way jiggy little shred when snow and mud clog Northern AZ trails. Set rockets to burn and dial the assault-mobile ride finder for Dead Horse Ranch.

Cottonwood is much too dang hot in summer, but deee-lightful the rest of the year. The exquisite Tuzigoot ruins are only a skip and a hop away. Fishing is great. Campsites are plentiful. Do Thumper either way, but clockwise is best. Climb the 2-track and descend single track. Mo-betta-go-fast fun that way.

The Verde is one of the desert's last free flowing rivers sustaining a lush and large plant and wildlife population. Verde River Greenway is a critical six-mile stretch of The Verde renown for its many natural and cultural resources. Dead Horse Ranch State Park anchors that greenway. You gotta pop for one dead prez to get in.

### MILEAGE LOG

0.0 Follow Thumper map to START. Go around the gate. After 0.1 mile, take the single track on your RIGHT. Go up steep as trail becomes gnarly jeep 2-track.
2.8 "T" junction. Go RIGHT.
3.0 Right at fork. Singletrack next. Go down Thumper.
5.1 Thumper meets Lime Kiln Trail. Go Right.
7.2 Pavement. Go RIGHT back to trailhead.
8.0 Back to GO. Need more? Ride up Raptor again, go LEFT at the top and head down Bones Trail. There is a tough 1- track descent to Pecks Lake and Tuzigoot. Makes a loop to Cottonwood and a 21 mile total day.

*"Getting old is when it takes longer to recover than it did to do the damage."*
*-ANDREI CORDRESCU*

COTTONWOOD

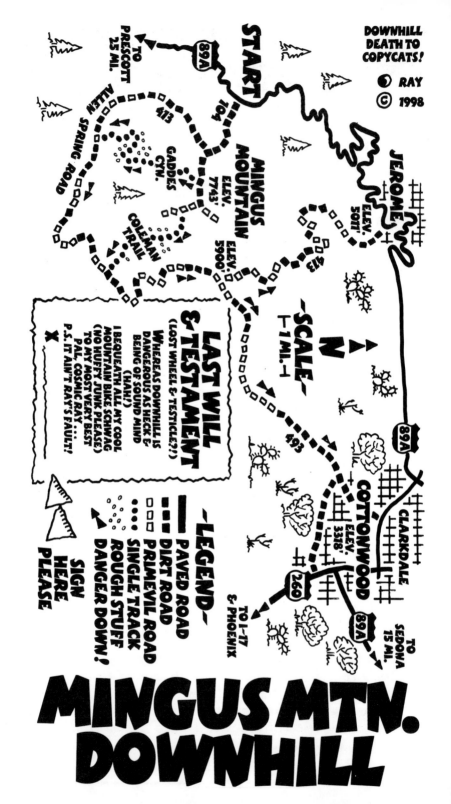

DOWNHILL
DEATH TO
COPYCATS!

◑ RAY
© 1998

# MINGUS MTN. DOWNHILL

# Cottonwood ☠ MINGUS MTN ☠
## WICKED DOWNHILL

**DISTANCE:** 21 MILES
**TIME:** 1.5 to 3 HOURS
**EFFORT:** ALL DOWNHILL
**SKILL:** EXPERT DH
**PUCK-O-METER:** PUCK 10
WARP SPEED DESCENT
**FIND ROUTE:** CAKE
**SEASON:** APR to NOV

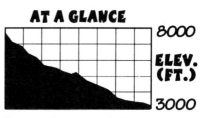

**AT A GLANCE**

8000

**ELEV. (FT.)**

3000

O  **1-WAY MILES**  21

**I FIND IT DISGUSTING AND IMMORAL** to use internal combustion other than one's own intestinal fortitude to get *up* a hill just to roll one's lazy fat arse *down* the hill. However, the idea of a 21 mile descent appeals to my OTHER self. My *BAD DOG* self. Don't tell anyone I suggested this. It is *WRONG!* You can suffer excruciatingly painful injuries OR you may get lucky and merely die. My buddy Vito Stamata flipped up a rock at speed, augered big time and gave up mountain biking for good. Let that be a lesson. Kiss the dog, pat the family good bye and go full face helmet plus full freaking body armor.

**ALLEN SPRING ROAD:** This is the BIG downhill. I do not suggest you do this, merely that a curiosity may exist about a hypothetical route. See the map. It's 21 sensational big ring miles DOWN a dirt road from the top of Mingus above Jerome to Cottonwood. It's all downhill except for a teeny tiny 2 minute climb in the middle.

**COLEMAN TRAIL:** I call it Suicide Trail, but the USFS says it's OK so it must be OK. Start your Mingus downhill run with a little technical hairball single track. This 1.8 mile short cut jumps off the top of Mingus to Allen Spring Road. To access GO 2.6 miles on FS104 to campground. FORK RIGHT on 104A in the campground then 0.5 miles to launch at the radio towers. Front and rear suspension and a big pillow on your seat reccomended.

**GADDES CANYON TRAIL:** Another single track short cut to start the Mingus downhill. This 2.3 mile twister to Allen Spring Road. starts technical then turns sweet and swift near the end. From HWY 89 Take FS 104 2.25 miles to 104B junction. Take 104B to 0.1 miles before the lookout. Trailhead is on the left. Again, full bounce!

*"Go fast. Take chances."*
*- yet more stupid irresponsible advice*

COTTONWOOD

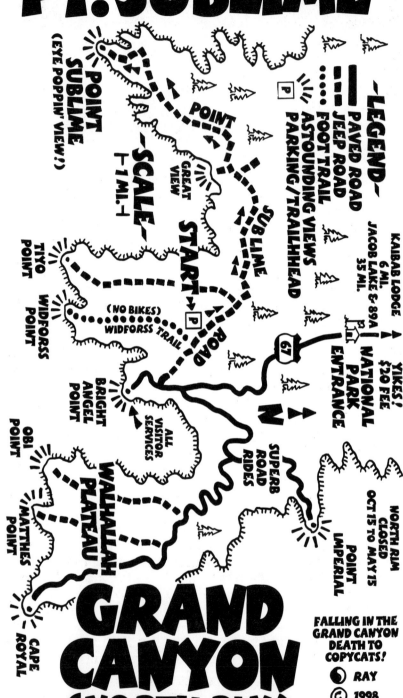

# PT. SUBLIME

**POINT SUBLIME**
(EYE POPPIN' VIEW!)

**—LEGEND—**
PAVED ROAD
JEEP ROAD
FOOT TRAIL
ASTOUNDING VIEWS
P PARKING/TRAILHEAD

KAIBAB LODGE
6 MI.
JACOB LAKE & 89A
35 MI.

**—SCALE—**
⊢ 1 MI. ⊣

POINT
SUBLIME

GREAT
VIEW

START →

YIKES!
$20 FEE

NATIONAL
PARK
ENTRANCE

67

N

(NO BIKES)
WIDFORSS TRAIL

TIYO
POINT

WIDFORSS
POINT

A ROAD

BRIGHT
ANGEL
POINT

ALL
VISITOR
SERVICES

SUPERB
ROAD
RIDES

NORTH RIM
CLOSED
OCT 15 TO MAY 15

POINT
IMPERIAL

OBI
POINT

WALHALLA
PLATEAU

MATTHES
POINT

CAPE
ROYAL

# GRAND CANYON (NORTH RIM)

FALLING IN THE
GRAND CANYON
DEATH TO
COPYCATS!

◐ RAY

© 1998

# Grand Canyon POINT SUBLIME
## NORTH RIM TRAIL TO SUBLIME VIEW

**DISTANCE:** 36 MILES R.T.
**TIME:** 6 HOURS
**EFFORT:** VERY LONG RIDE
**SKILL:** EASY
**PUCK-O-METER:** PUCK 3
  LONG, EASY DIRT ROAD TO VIEW
**FIND ROUTE:** EASY
**SEASON:** MAY to OCT

**AT A GLANCE**

9500

ELEV.
(FT.)

7000

O  **1-WAY MILES**  18

**DESCRIPTION:** The North Rim sits on a huge thumb of land jutting into The Canyon called The Kaibab Plateau. Sweet smelling old growth pines tower 200 ft. above a silent forest floor. The height and girth of the old growth ponderosas make you feel just a bit wee.

A rough jeep road runs all the way to Point Sublime through sunny meadows and forest. The first 10 miles roll up and down gaining 500 ft. until gradually descending 1,000 ft. to Pt. Sublime. Be sure to check out a great view and photo op about 5 miles before Pt. Sublime. No food or water available along the way. Bring rain gear during the summer monsoon season. Caution, the rescue index on this little travelled road is near zero.

Grand Canyon National Park is struggling to keep up with the burden of over 5 million visitors per year. Plans are afoot at the South Rim for a light rail and closing the park to cars. Included is a bike/foot trail all along the South Rim. Yipee! However, that's 5 years down the road. Meanwhile all dirt roads in the park are closed to bikes except Point Sublime. Camping is limited to the park campground. Reserve way in advance. Free dry camping in nearby Kaibab National Forest is easy. Showers, laundry, food, gas, meals, espresso, trinkets and all that brouhaha are found at North Rim Village inside the national park.

**DIRECTIONS:** Easy to find. Go 2.7 miles north of Grand Canyon North Rim Lodge and west at the sign "Widfross Trailhead". Go 1 mile to the parking area and start there.

*"The life of the land is preserved in the righteousness of the people."*
*-Hawaii's very cool state motto*

**GRAND CYN**

# RAINBOW RIM

○ RAY
© 1998

GRAND CANYON

PARISSAWAMPITTS POINT
BRING BINOCS
START

FENCE POINT
LITTLE FENCE

NATURAL ARCH
LOCUST POINT

N →

TIMP POINT
LITTLE TIMP
NORTH TIMP

271A

271

294

293

250

214

250

─SCALE─
⊤ 1/2 MI. ⊢

─LEGEND─
▬▬▬ PAVED
■ ■ ■ DIRT
□ □ □ PRIMITIVE
• • • • SINGLE TRACK
Ⓣ TRAILHEAD

## GETTING THERE

FIND THE TOWN OF JACOB LAKE AT THE
NORTH RIM OF THE GRAND CANYON
ON ANY ARIZONA HIWAY ROAD MAP.
GO SOUTH ON HIWAY 67 TOWARD THE
NATIONAL PARK ENTRANCE FOR 27 MILES TO
MILEPOST 605.9 (1 MILE PAST KAIBAB LODGE).
TURN RIGHT ON FS 22 AND FOLLOW THE SIGNS
22 MILES TO "VISTA POINTS".

# GRAND CANYON (NORTH RIM)

# *Grand Canyon* RAINBOW RIM TRAIL
## SINGLE TRACK RIGHT ON THE RIM

**DISTANCE:** 18 MILES 1 WAY
**TIME:** ALL DAY LONG
**EFFORT:** HARD WORK
**SKILL:** FAIRLY EASY
**PUCK-O-METER:** PUCK 3
GOOD TRAIL AWAY FROM THE EDGE
**FIND ROUTE:** EASY
**SEASON:** MAY 15 to OCT. 15

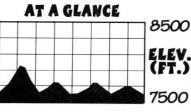

AT A GLANCE

8500

ELEV. (FT.)

7500

0    1-WAY MILES    18

PRIMO

TRAIL

**DESCRIPTION:** YES! At last you can ride your mountain bike along the very rim edge of of the Grand Canyon. Picture the North Rim as a giant thumb sticking out into The Canyon from the Kaibab Plateau. Along an 18 mile stretch of the western edge of that thumb, the Kaibab National Forest has constructed 18 miles of new single track.

Rainbow Rim Trail has been set with a small track machine and lots of hand labor anticipating that, as pine needles fall and native plants grow in, it will mature to a fine single track with a natural look and feel. They built the trail with bikes in mind. *VERY COOL! THANK YOU!*

Along the Rainbow Rim sets a series of five points sticking out into the abyss. The trail connects these as it meanders back up drainages to avoid steep changes in elevation, then back out to the next point. All this makes for constantly changing perspectives and killer views over humongo Tapeats Amphitheater containing whole mountains, canyons, terraces, buttes, spires and castles all in purple, verdant greens and shades of crimson.

The main trailheads are located either end at Parissawampitts Point and Timp Point, but the trail can be accessed at any point along the way. The roads are not great, but they can be negotiated in a 2WD car. You may camp free at any of the points. There is no water or food along the way. Bring rain gear for summer monsoon.

North Rim roads **OPEN MAY 15 AND CLOSE OCT 15** as snow arrives early and stays late in the far northern Arizona high country.

GRAND CYN

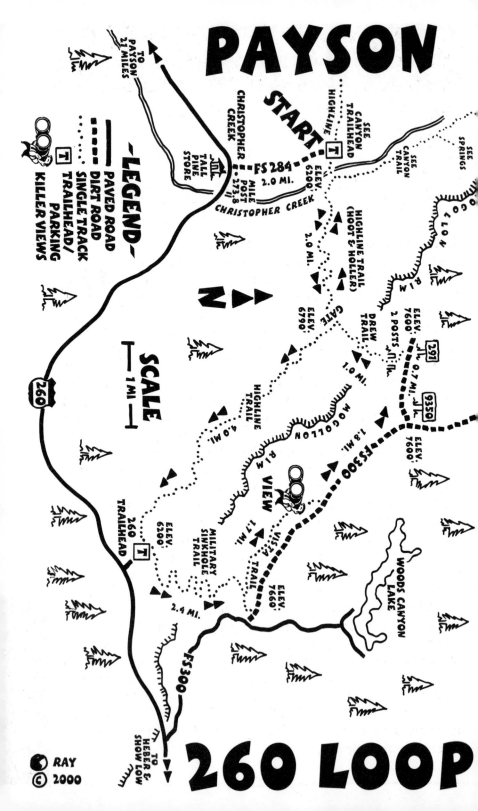

# PAYSON

# 260 LOOP

-LEGEND-

PAVED ROAD
DIRT ROAD
SINGLE TRACK
TRAILHEAD/ PARKING
KILLER VIEWS

SCALE
1 MI.

N

START

TO PAYSON 21 MILES

CHRISTOPHER CREEK

TALL PINE STORE

SEE CANYON TRAILHEAD

SEE CANYON TRAIL

SEE SPRINGS

FS 284 2.0 MI.

ELEV. 6200'

MILE POST 273.8

CHRISTOPHER CREEK

HIGHLINE TRAILHEAD

HIGHLINE TRAIL (HOOT & HOLLER)

2.0 MI.

ELEV. 6790'

GATE

DREW TRAIL

2 POSTS

1.0 MI.

ELEV. 7600'

291

9350

ELEV. 7600'

FS 300

1.8 MI.

MOGOLLON RIM

HIGHLINE TRAIL

4.0 MI.

260 TRAILHEAD

ELEV. 6200'

VIEW

VISTA TRAIL

1.7 MI.

MILITARY SINKHOLE TRAIL

1.7 MI.

ELEV. 7660'

WOODS CANYON LAKE

2.4 MI.

FS 300

TO HEBER & SHOW LOW

RAY
© 2000

# Payson 260 (HILINE TRAIL) LOOP
## "BEST SINGLE TRACK IN THE STATE."

**DISTANCE:** 15.6 MILES
**TIME:** 3 HOURS OR SO
**EFFORT:** TOUGH
**SKILL:** ADVANCED
**PUCK-O-METER:** PUCK 8
HIGH SPEED TWISTY DESCENTS
**FIND ROUTE:** EASY
**SEASON:** APR to NOV

**AT A GLANCE**

8000

**ELEV. (FT.)**

5500

O    **LOOP MILES**    15.6

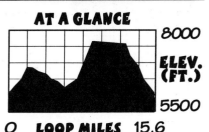

**DESCRIPTION:** This is *the* cheap thrills stretch of infamous old #31 Highline Trail and then some. Creep up thru giant old timber onto the Mogollon (say Moe-ghee-own!) Rim. Follow along rim views clear to The Mazatzal Mountains. Dive down thru a fern forest, careful not to sample the salad bar. Do this loop counter-clockwise only or be lost and out all night. On "Hoot n' Holler" descent (see map), *Rim Country Mountain Biking* says "best single track in the state". It's a big state, but I just might have to agree!

**DIRECTIONS:** EASY TO FOLLOW. YOU CAN DO THIS LOOP JUST FROM THE MAP, BUT BE SURE TO GET OFF ON THE RIGHT FOOT FROM THE GET GO! HEED PAYSON EXPERT JOHN LAKE'S WORDS . . .

"From See Canyon Trailhead (see map) take the trail that is just to your RIGHT as you pull into the parking lot and work your way down to the creek. Dismount as you cross the creek. The trail is straight ahead, slightly to the right and forks in about 50 yards. Go RIGHT. This is the Highline (Hoot & Holler) Trail . . . two miles of lung busting, switchback maneuvering, root hopping, rock dodging fun up through old growth forest. Remember, what goes up *will* come down later. Average riders take 30 minutes to cover this first section.

Remember, get on the proper trail in the first place. At the very beginning it might help to follow the diamond markers nailed to trees. Once past that first See Canyon/Highline Trail fork, the rest of the loop is super easy to follow." Right on, John Lake. Thank you!

**PAYSON**

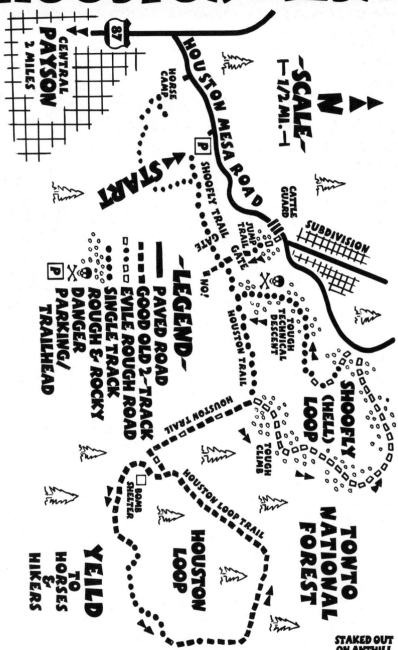

# Payson HOUSTON MESA
## TWO FUN LOOP TRAILS CLOSE TO TOWN

**DISTANCE:** 5 to 10 MILES
**TIME:** 2 to 3 HOURS
**EFFORT:** MODERATE
**SKILL:** INTERMEDIATE
**PUCK-O-METER:** NO PUCK
**FIND ROUTE:** MODERATE
**SEASON:** ALL YEAR

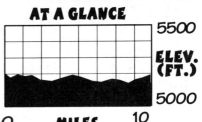

**AT A GLANCE**

5500

ELEV. (FT.)

5000

O          MILES          10

**DESCRIPTION:** Densely forested with pinyon, juniper and manzanita, verdant Houston Mesa is Payson's very best close-in place to ride. The Houston Loop single track and rolling old 2-track is favored by intermediate riders looking for trails on public land close to town. Rough, steep and technical Shoofly is suitable only for full boing thrill and pain seekers looking for goodness-knows-what.

Houston's crushed granite soil drains well and hooks up great wet or dry. Shoofly Loop's rough jeep road and single track clay turn heinous gummy glue when wet. Both loops are about 5 miles each plus the ride in.

**DIRECTIONS:** Head north 2 miles from Manzanita Cycles in Payson on HWY 87. Turn Right on Houston Mesa Road and go another mile to the Houston Mesa Trailhead on the right. These national forest trails are well marked, but if you get confused just follow the signs that say "horse camp" and they will lead you back to the trailhead.

PAYSON

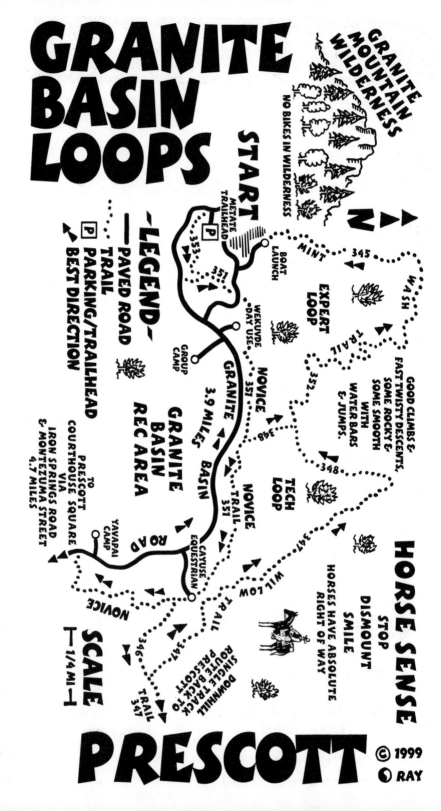

# Prescott GRANITE BASIN LOOPS
## GREAT LOOPS FOR ALL ABILITY LEVELS

**DISTANCE:** 12 PLUS MILES OF SINGLE TRACK LOOPS
**TIME:** 2 TO 3 HOURS OR MUCH MORE IF YOU LIKE
**EFFORT:** MANY EASY TO DIFFICULT LOOP TRAILS
**SKILL:** ROOKIE TO ADVANCED
**FIND ROUTE:** MOST TRAILS ARE SIGNED, BUT THE AREA HAS *MORE* TRAILS THAN SHOWN ON MAP
**SEASON:** SOME SNOW IN WINTER

**DESCRIPTION:** A loop for rank beginners and lots more for the rest of us . . . fast, rough, smooth, twisty-turny single track with jumps, rocks, bumps, hops, hard packed soil and a little exposure here and there to add spice. In short, everything, all great. If you rode out, there's a secret mostly downhill single track back to town. See the map.

This is a Prescott National Forest Recreation Area. Lots of folks recreating here. There's a cool little lake. Good for kids. Be courteous and share the trails. Use special caution around horses. Stop, dismount, smile. Especially smile. It won't kill ya to schmooze a little with the horse people and keep the good vibe going.

**DIRECTIONS:** From downtown Courthouse Square go northwest on Montezuma Street and continue as it becomes Iron Springs Road and heads out of town. After you've gone 4.7 miles turn right on Granite Basin Road and go 3.9 miles to Metate Trailhead. $2 fee to park the The Beast. Too much? Ride part way out and ride free.

**PRESCOTT**

# SPRUCE MTN.

TO PRESCOTT
(MT. VERNON ST.)
6.0 MI.

**N**

**-SCALE-**
⊢ 1/2 MI. ⊣

**-LEGEND-**
—— PAVED ROAD
- - - DIRT ROAD
· · · SINGLE TRACK
Ⓟ PARKING/
TRAILHHEAD

SENATOR HWY.

0.6 MI.

SPRUCE MOUNTAIN ROAD

DIRT ROAD WAY UP

GROOM CREEK

TRAIL 307 — 1.0 MI.

START

ELEV. 6360'

Ⓟ

TRAIL 307
STEEP & FAST
WAY UP

**PLEASE NOTE!**
PROTECT TRAIL ACCESS.
CONTROL YOUR SPEED.
HORSES AND HIKERS HAVE
RIGHT OF WAY.

LOOK OUT

VIEW

STEEP UP
GRUNT CITY!

3.5 MI.

TRAIL 307

STEEP UP
HURT!

ELEV. 7693'

TRAIL 307

TRAIL 307

SENATOR HWY.

5.5 MI.

YOW! IT'S THE BITCHIN' DESCENT!

TO CROWN KING

# PRESCOTT

DEATH TO
COPYCATS!

🌀 RAY
ⓒ 1998

**DISTANCE:** 9 MILES
**TIME:** 2 HOURS
**EFFORT:** WHAT GOES UP...
**SKILL:** ADVANCED
**PUCK-O-METER:** PUCK 9
MACH 9 DESCENT WITH SOME DEBRIS
**FIND ROUTE:** E-Z
**SEASON:** APR to NOV

**AT A GLANCE**

8500

**ELEV. (FT.)**

6000

O    **LOOP MILES**    9

**DESCRIPTION:** Nine miles of the best . . . killer views, smooth line, banked turns, way steep and deep ravines. Miss a turn, next stop Groom Creek! Weekdays best. Horse people work! AM weekends are worst.

PRIMO TRAIL

From the parking lot it's easy up for the first miles then a wall near the top. The lookout is 0.1 miles from the top of #307. Find a sittin' rock and scope some eye poppin' views. North see The Frisco Peaks beyond Flagstaff. In front of The Peaks is Mingus Mountain. West is a bird's eye view of Prescott. South set the Bradshaws. Finally, rip airborne express 5.5 miles down the bitchin' single track descent. Spruce Mountain gets snow in winter and may be a little rough after spring snowmelt or summer monsoon rain.

**DIRECTIONS:** Easy. From Courthouse Square go 0.6 miles east on E.Gurley. RIGHT on S.Mt.Vernon St. (Senator Hiway). Groom Creek is at 6.6 miles and Trail #307 trailhead is on the left a mile past Groom Creek. If road turns dirt, you blew the turn.

## MILEAGE LOG

0.0 CLOCKWISE is best so head LEFT up #307.

1.9 TRAIL SPLITS. Brain in neutral. LEFT and UP. Ugh!

3.3 TOP of #307. Look out from lookout then DESCEND with care not to die or waste a horse.

9.0 BACK TO BOTTOM. Wipe that cheezy grin off your gub. Try it again in the other direction. It's an itty bitty gear, tech roll up the twisty single track before streaking the lightning descent. Trail rash special. Watch for horses!

PRESCOTT

# Prescott THUMB BUTTE TRAILS
## LOTSA FUN OPTIONS WITHIN LOOP ROAD

**DISTANCE:** LOOP TRAIL OPTIONS 3 TO 20 MILES
**EFFORT:** NOTHING SUPER TOUGH
**SKILL:** ALL LEVELS OF ABILITY
**FEAR:** BEWARE THE CARS ON THUMB BUTTE ROAD
**FIND ROUTE:** SOME SIGNED, SOME NOT
**SEASON:** ALL YEAR (SNOW POSSIBLE IN WINTER)

**DESCRIPTION:** Spot Thumb Butte from anywhere in Prescott looking west. Huge, thumb-like rockpile marks the town's closest-in, best riding and hiking.

A G.P.S. survey ride reveals too many trails to show on a single map (Looks like a plate of linguini!) , thus only main trails are shown to provide a basis for exploration. You are always within Thumb Butte *Loop* Road, so you can't get too lost. You always come out somewhere, but a compass might come in handy if you like to feel safe.

At 7000', Thumb Butte Road's high point is the expansive Sierra Prieta Overlook to Copper Basin and beyond to the west. FS 51 bisects the loop road with a quiet roll through the forest. There are many, many other 4WD roads and trails within the loop that are great to find yourself although they have been known to miners and ranchers for over 100 years. Thumb Butte Loop Road is nearly all busy dirt road. Too many cars.

**DIRECTIONS:** From Courthouse Square go west on Gurley St. This runs onto Thumb Butte Road. It now cost $2 to park a car here, so ride the 3 miles from town.

**PRESCOTT**

# WHITE ROCK
## (ROCK PAINTED WHITE)
# LOOP TRAILS

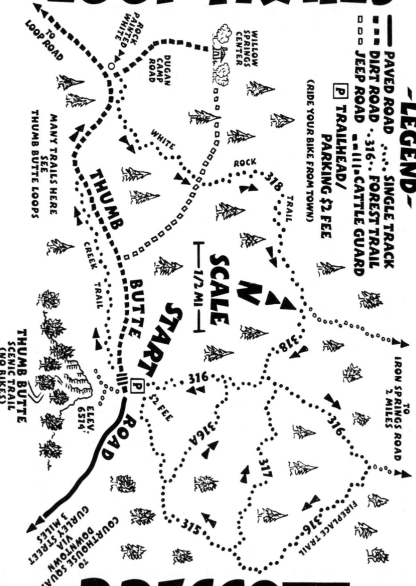

~LEGEND~

PAVED ROAD ▬ SINGLE TRACK
DIRT ROAD •••• 316• FOREST TRAIL
JEEP ROAD ▢▢▢ •III• CATTLE GUARD

P TRAILHEAD/
PARKING $2 FEE
(RIDE YOUR BIKE FROM TOWN)

TO LOOP ROAD
ROCK PAINTED WHITE
DUGAN CAMP ROAD
WILLOW SPRINGS CENTER
WHITE
ROCK
318 TRAIL
MANY TRAILS HERE SEE THUMB BUTTE LOOPS
THUMB
BUTTE
CREEK TRAIL
SCALE
N
1/2 MI
318
START
$2 FEE
316
316A
316
317
316
315
IRON SPRINGS ROAD 2 MILES
FIREPLACE TRAIL
THUMB BUTTE SCENIC TRAIL (NO BIKES)
ELEV. 6514'
ROAD
TO COURTHOUSE SQUARE DOWNTOWN VIA GURLEY STREET 3 MILES

# PRESCOTT

Ⓡ RAY
© 1999

# Prescott WHITE ROCK LOOPS
## VERY FUN SINGLE TRACK LOOP TRAILS

**DISTANCE:** 12 PLUS SINGLE TRACK LOOP MILES
**TIME:** 2 HOURS AND CHANGE
**EFFORT:** ALL MODERATE ROLLING SINGLE TRACK
**SKILL:** VERY ENTERTAINING INTERMEDIATE
**FEAR:** GO FAST, TAKE CHANCES
**FIND ROUTE:** MOSTLY SIGNED, BUT NOT ALL
**SEASON:** ALL YEAR (SNOW POSSIBLE IN WINTER)

**DESCRIPTION:** I had a great time trying to hang on to my pal Josh's rear wheel . . . and he was on a single speed. Nothing too steep or deep. All very fun, ripping, rolling, jumping single track located just across the road from Thumb Butte. In about 2 hours time, we rode every inch of single track trail in the immediate area. My odometer said 12 plus miles at the end. Trails are mostly signed with numbers, but not all turns are marked. Bring the map and compass if it makes you feel mo' betta.

Start your loops at Thumb Butte parking area. If you drive from town, it'll cost ya two bones to park. Head up the creek trail across the road. See map. Climb up to the small Rock Painted White that marks Dugan Camp Road. The single track descent and loops begin here. This is fun stuff, but if it isn't enough, turn the page, cross the road and check out Thumb Butte Loop Trails.

**DIRECTIONS:** Go 3 miles from Courthouse Square on Gurley Street. Gurley becomes Thumb Butte Road. If you drive, avoid $2 fee. Park somewhere along the way. Fry's is a good bet to park and ride. And it has a bakery.

PRESCOTT

# *Prescott* **WOLF CREEK LOOP**
## SMOOTH JEEP ROAD ALONG CREEK

**DISTANCE:** 4.6 MILE LOOP
**TIME:** 1 TO 1.5 HOURS
**EFFORT:** FAIRLY EASY
**SKILL:** ROOKIE RIDE
**PUCK-O-METER:** PUCK 5
    JUST ONE FAST DIRT DESCENT
**FIND ROUTE:** ALL SIGNED
**SEASON:** APR TO NOV

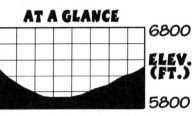

**AT A GLANCE**

6800

**ELEV. (FT.)**

5800

O   **LOOP MILES**  4.6

**DESCRIPTION:** This easy, short loop drops down to a sparkling little stream with plenty of places to picnic, sunbathe or sploosh around in the shallows. It's a good stout ride for kids too and not without some uphill. From the start where you park your car, you drop about 400 feet over 2 miles to the Hassayampa River. You begin a good climb back up as soon as you leave the river. What goes down must go up, ya know, but walking ain't no crime. Part of the descent is over a smooth, but braided crushed granite surface. It can be slippery and a bit tricky for a novice. Use the big levers on your handle bars. They work great for speed control.

    Note that The Hassayampa usually flows at just a trickle, but during times of runoff it can be big and bad. Use some judgement when goofing off around water.

**DIRECTIONS:** You can ride from town, but for most beginners the 6 mile climb up to Groom Creek is a bit much. Anyway, from Courthouse Square go 0.6 miles east on E. Gurley then RIGHT on Mt. Vernon. Continue as it becomes Senator Highway through Groom Creek.

## MILEAGE LOG

0.0 Park and START where Senator Highway turns dirt. Go right onto signed FS 97.
1.1 LEFT through Lower Wolf Creek Campground. FS 74 begins at the rear of the campground. Caution, the descent is quick and somewhat tricky.
2.3 LEFT and CONTINUE along creek heading upstream.
3.0 LEFT onto FS 79 and head uphill away from creek.
4.4 LEFT onto Senator Highway. Watch for cars.
4.6 Back to GO. Now wasn't that easy?

**PRESCOTT**

# SHOW LOW
## (WHITE MOUNTAINS)

### DIRECTIONS

FROM SHOW LOW GO EAST ON HWY 60 TOWARD SPRINGERVILLE FOR 19 MILES. GO RIGHT AT VERNON ON FOREST ROAD 224 ANOTHER 9 MILES TO LOS BURROS.

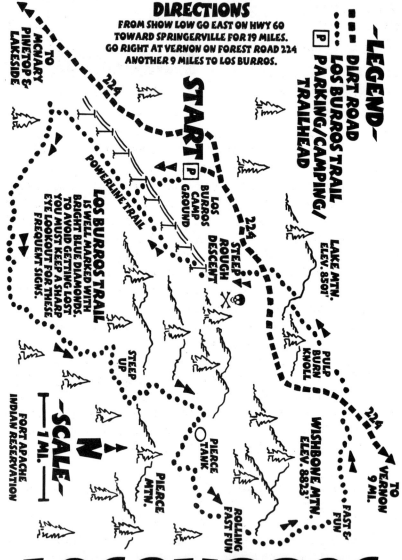

**-LEGEND-**

- ■ ■ ■ DIRT ROAD
- • • • LOS BURROS TRAIL
- Ⓟ PARKING/CAMPING/ TRAILHEAD

TO McNARY PINETOP & LAKESIDE

224

START

Ⓟ LOS BURROS CAMP GROUND

224

STEEP & ROUGH DESCENT

POWERLINE TRAIL

LOS BURROS TRAIL IS WELL MARKED WITH BRIGHT BLUE DIAMONDS. TO AVOID GETTING LOST YOU MUST KEEP A SHARP EYE LOOKOUT FOR THESE FREQUENT SIGNS.

LAKE MTN. ELEV. 8501'

PULP BURN KNOLL

224 TO VERNON 9 MI.

STEEP UP

FORT APACHE INDIAN RESERVATION

SCALE 1 MI.

N

PIERCE TANK

PIERCE MTN.

WISHBONE MTN. ELEV. 8823'

ROLLING FAST FUN

FAST & FUN

# LOS BURROS LOOP

SUCKING MUD DEATH TO COPYCATS!

Ⓒ RAY Ⓒ 1998

# Show Low: LOS BURROS TRAIL
## SUPERB SINGLE TRACK LOOP

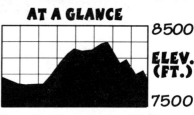

**DISTANCE:** 13.5 MILES
**TIME:** 1.5 to 2.5 HOURS
**EFFORT:** NOT TOO TOUGH
**SKILL:** INTERMEDIATE
**PUCK-O-METER:** NO ALARM
**FIND ROUTE:** MODERATE
**SEASON:** APR to OCT

**AT A GLANCE**

8500
**ELEV. (FT.)**
7500

O **LOOP MILES** 13.5

**DESCRIPTION:** I reckon this hoot and holler rolling single track loop to be the very best fat tire ride in the White Mountains. That's what all the local dirtheads say and I have to agree. There's one good tough climb and many twisty turny descents through towering old growth pine and aspen forest plus you really get a feeling that you're in an as yet undiscovered part of the state. I had a great time here.

PRIMO

TRAIL

The White Mountains are the closest thing Arizona has to a rain forest. The winter storm track dips down over eastern Arizona to dump loads of snow and the summer monsoon keeps the forest floor damp and cool, yet mud does not seem to be a problem. The soil is made of mostly soft forest humus rather than that icky clay stuff that sticks to your tires and makes you go postal.

The Los Burros Loop is maintained and well marked. If you go more than 100 yards without seeing a diamond nailed to a tree, you are headed in the wrong direction and should backtrack to the last marker. Lotsa tire tracks to follow too.

**DIRECTIONS:** From Show Low go 19 miles east on HWY 60 toward Springerville then RIGHT at Vernon onto FS224. Continue 10 miles to Los Burros Camground and trailhead. From Phoenix take HWY 170 via Globe to Pinetop-Lakeside and Show Low. It's about a 3 hour drive.

**OPTIONS:** Los Burros is part of the White Mountains Trail System, a dozen nearby connected trails. Get a free copy of the superb White Mountains Trail System Guide free from the USFS in Lakeside (520) 368-5111.

**WHITE MTNS**

# BROWN CANYON LOOP

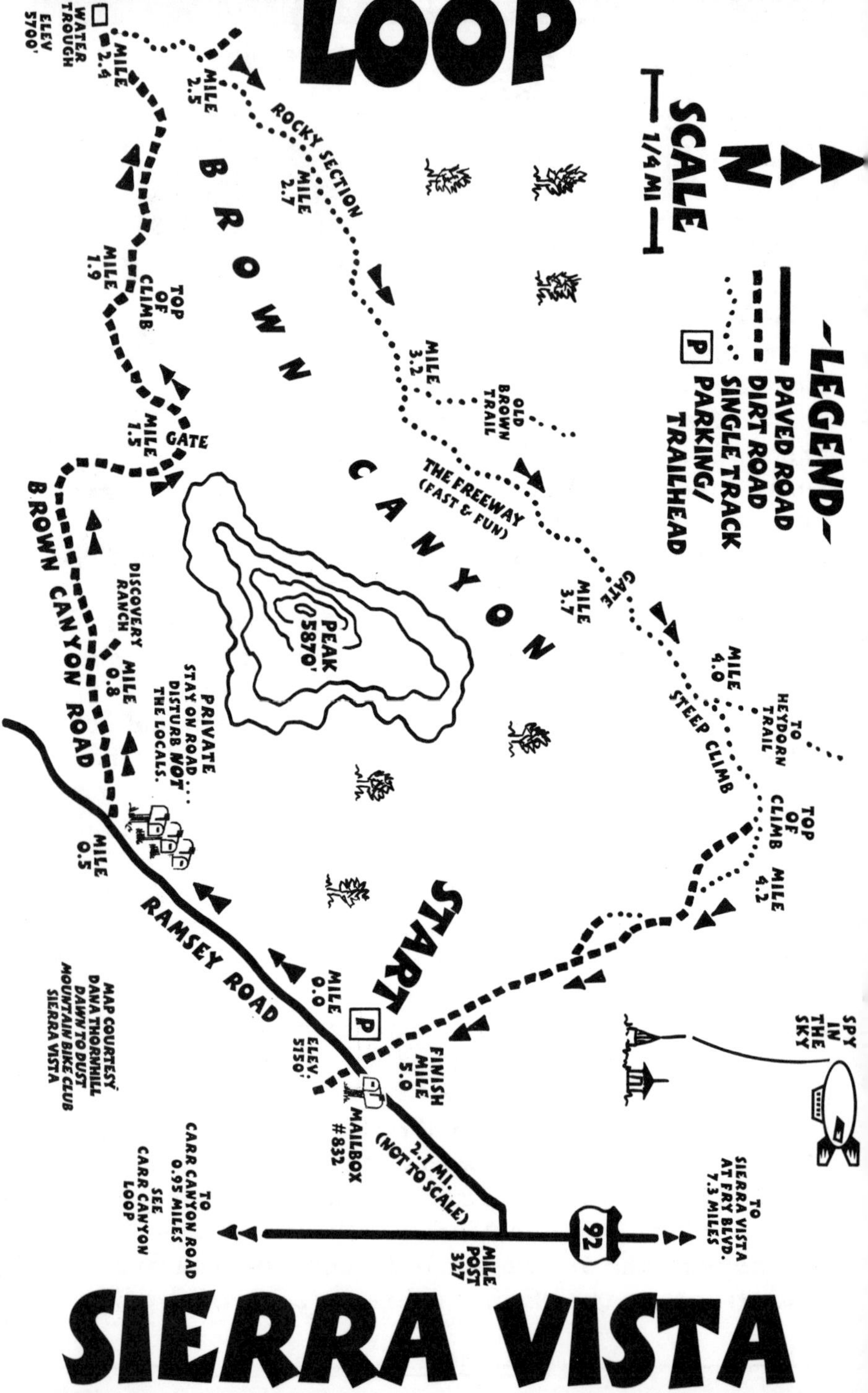

## SIERRA VISTA

**SCALE**
1/4 MI

**N**

**-LEGEND-**

PAVED ROAD

DIRT ROAD

SINGLE TRACK

P  PARKING/
TRAILHEAD

WATER TROUGH
ELEV 5700'
MILE 2.4
MILE 2.5
ROCKY SECTION
MILE 2.7
MILE 1.9
TOP OF CLIMB
MILE 1.5
GATE

BROWN CANYON

OLD BROWN TRAIL
MILE 3.2
THE FREEWAY (FAST & FUN)
MILE 3.7
GATE

BROWN CANYON ROAD

DISCOVERY RANCH
MILE 0.8

PRIVATE
STAY ON ROAD...
DISTURB *NOT*
THE LOCALS.

PEAK 5870'

MILE 0.5

RAMSEY ROAD

MILE 0.0
ELEV 5150'

START

P

MAILBOX #832

TO HEYDORN TRAIL
MILE 4.0
STEEP CLIMB
TOP OF CLIMB MILE 4.2

FINISH MILE 5.0

2.1 MI. (NOT TO SCALE)

SPY IN THE SKY

TO SIERRA VISTA AT FRY BLVD. 7.3 MILES

MAP COURTESY
DAWN THORNHILL
DAWN TO DUST
MOUNTAIN BIKE CLUB
SIERRA VISTA

TO CARR CANYON ROAD 0.95 MILES
SEE CARR CANYON LOOP

92

MILE POST 327

# Sierra Vista: BROWN CANYON LOOP
## FUN SINGLE TRACK DESCENT

**DISTANCE:** 5 MILES
**TIME:** 1 HOUR
**EFFORT:** MODERATE
**SKILL:** JUST A BIT
**PUCK-O-METER:** PUCK 7.5
    HIGH SPEED DESCENT
**FIND ROUTE:** MODERATE
**SEASON:** SEP to JUN

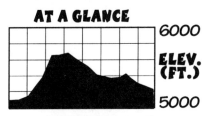

**AT A GLANCE**

6000

**ELEV. (FT.)**

5000

O    **LOOP MILES**    5

**DESCRIPTION:** A big fave among the locals. Zoom down to Sierra Vista for a day of muy rapido 1-track action. Brown combines with Carr Canyon Loop. Turn the page to Carr and check it out. Between the two loops and the road connection, you'll milk it for 20 miles with the bulk being single track descent. Brown Loop climbs a gnurly 2-track jeep road and gains about 500' in a couple of miles. Then get airborne for a flying 2.5 mile rip down a whoop-de-doo trail interrupted only by one short grunt climb.

Check out the border patrol mini-blimp tethered high overhead watching your every paranoid move. This trusty robotic eye guards for dope and aliens pouring across the border. I don't know about you, but to me nothing says inner peace like a big eyeball in the sky. It's a weird, weird world, but a great ride regardless.

**DIRECTIONS:** Head south out of Sierra Vista on HWY 92 for about 7 miles to milepost 327. Turn RIGHT onto Ramsey Canyon Road and go 2.1 miles to mailbox #832. Trailhead parking area is just across the road. The first half mile of this loop is paved. As soon as you turn right on dirt Brown Canyon Road, you are going through private property for a quarter mile or so. Stay on the road, follow your nose and mind your own beezwax. Do not disturb the locals and they will not disturb you. They are mostly cool, but you never know.

SIERRA VISTA

# SIERRA VISTA

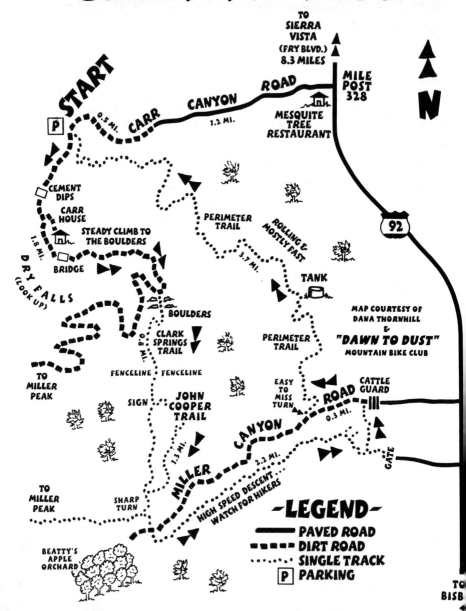

TO SIERRA VISTA (FRY BLVD.) 8.3 MILES

START

CARR CANYON ROAD

0.5 MI.

1.2 MI.

MILE POST 328

MESQUITE TREE RESTAURANT

P

CEMENT DIPS

CARR HOUSE

STEADY CLIMB TO THE BOULDERS

1.8 MI.

DRY FALLS (LOOK UP)

BRIDGE

PERIMETER TRAIL

ROLLING & MOSTLY FAST

3.7 MI.

92

TANK

BOULDERS

CLARK SPRINGS TRAIL

0.8 MI.

PERIMETER TRAIL

MAP COURTESY OF DANA THORNHILL & "DAWN TO DUST" MOUNTAIN BIKE CLUB

TO MILLER PEAK

FENCELINE       FENCELINE

SIGN

JOHN COOPER TRAIL

1.3 MI.

EASY TO MISS TURN

ROAD

CATTLE GUARD

0.3 MI.

GATE

MILLER CANYON

2.2 MI.

TO MILLER PEAK

SHARP TURN

HIGH SPEED DESCENT WATCH FOR HIKERS

BEATTY'S APPLE ORCHARD

~LEGEND~

━━━━ PAVED ROAD
━ ━ ━ DIRT ROAD
‧‧‧‧‧‧ SINGLE TRACK
P PARKING

TO BISB

# CARR CANYON LOOP

N

# Sierra Vista: CARR CANYON LOOP
## BEST SINGLE TRACK RIDE IN TOWN

**DISTANCE:** 10 MILES
**TIME:** 2 to 3 HOURS
**EFFORT:** FAIRLY TOUGH
**SKILL:** ADVANCED
**PUCK-O-METER:** PUCK 7
SPEED AND EXPOSURE TO RISK
**FIND ROUTE:** MODERATE
**SEASON:** OCT to JUN

### AT A GLANCE

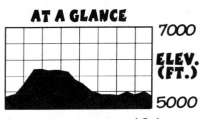

7000

**ELEV. (FT.)**

5000

O  **LOOP MILES**  10.1

**DESCRIPTION:** Gain gravity on a smooth dirt road that climbs up the foothills of the Huachuca Mountains then enjoy your earnings on a long, fast single track descent with lots of dips, twists, drops and a few surprises. Combine with Brown Canyon Loop to make the distance worth the 2-hour-south-of-Tucson drive to Sierra Vista.

### MILEAGE LOG

**0.0** Go south from Sierra Vista on HWY 92 for 8 miles to milepost 328. Go RIGHT on Carr Canyon Road another 1.7 miles. See 'da map. Park and ride uphill.

**1.8** Boulders mark LEFT turn onto 1-track. Fun begins! Lots of exposure to risk here. Good stuff!

**2.6** Sign marks John Cooper Trail. Go LEFT.

**3.9** Some quick turns. See map. STRAIGHT across Miller Canyon Road and begin speedy single track descent.

**6.1** Cattleguard. If you get to a gate, you blew the turn. At the cowguard Head back up Miller Canyon Road.

**6.4** Pay attention! Veeery sharp oblique RIGHT turn onto Perimeter Trail. More single track rolls up and down across several drainages back to the START.

**10.1** Back to GO. Next go visit Kartchner Caverns north of town if you made reservations and have time.

**SIERRA VISTA**

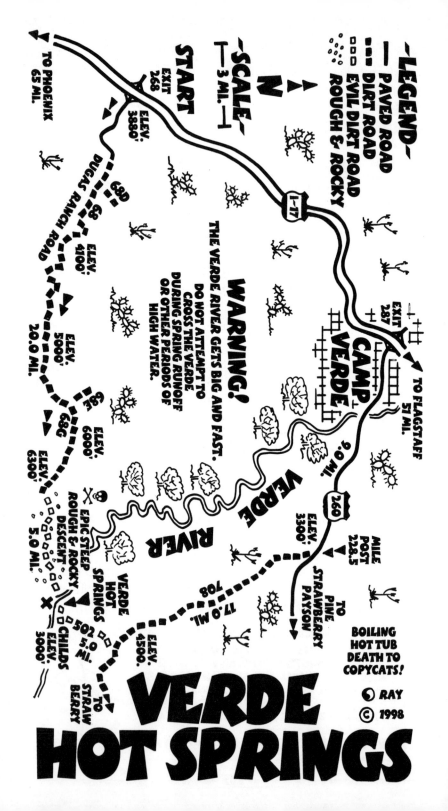

# VERDE HOT SPRINGS

—LEGEND—

| | PAVED ROAD |
| | DIRT ROAD |
| | EVIL DIRT ROAD |
| | ROUGH & ROCKY |

N

SCALE
3 MI.

START

EXIT 268
ELEV. 3880'

TO PHOENIX 65 MI.

68D

DUGAS RANCH ROAD

ELEV. 4100'

ELEV. 5000'

20.0 MI.

68E

68G

ELEV. 6000'

ELEV. 6300'

5.0 MI.

EPIC STEEP ROUGH & ROCKY DESCENT

VERDE HOT SPRINGS

502
5.0 MI.

CHILDS
ELEV. 3000'

TO STRAW BERRY

I-17

CAMP VERDE

EXIT 287

TO FLAGSTAFF 51 MI.

9.0 MI.

260

ELEV. 3300'

MILE POST 228.5

TO PINE STRAWBERRY PAYSON

VERDE RIVER

ELEV. 4500'

708

17.0 MI.

**WARNING!**
THE VERDE RIVER GETS BIG AND FAST. DO NOT ATTEMPT TO CROSS THE VERDE DURING SPRING RUNOFF OR OTHER PERIODS OF HIGH WATER.

BOILING HOT TUB DEATH TO COPYCATS!

RAY
© 1998

# VERDE HOT SPRINGS
## HISTORIC JEEP ROUTE TO HOT WATER

**DISTANCE:** 25 MILES
**TIME:** 4 HOURS
**EFFORT:** LONG RIDE
**SKILL:** ADVANCED
**PUCK-O-METER:** PUCK 9
ULTRA HAIRBALL DESCENT
**FIND ROUTE:** EASY
**SEASON:** MAR to NOV

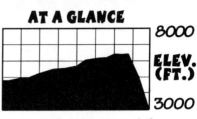

AT A GLANCE

8000

ELEV. (FT.)

3000

O   **1-WAY MILES**   25

**DESCRIPTION:** This buff-butt-ruff combines the best of all possible worlds . . . a long hard ride endingsteeply downhill into a pot of hot water. PLUS the Verde night sky reports more UFO activity than anywhere else in the world! UFOs? Yes, this be an unsolved mystery. This area is known for numerous uranium digs. Talk around the campfire in the scientific community has it that anything moving too fast to be seen on radar must be powered by, yup, you guessed it, uranium. Your hot tub pal may be on refueling furlough from another planet!

The springs quite hot. They are ruins of an old resort from days gone by. The resort burned, but the hot water remains. Do not drink the Verde River water. Camp Verde brown trout run these rapids. Bring water from home.

Arrange for your support to drop you at Dugas Road exit 268 on I-17. The shuttle zips to Camp Verde and down to the springs on FS 708 as shown on my so-called map. The shuttle carries water, bar-b-que, sleeping bags and brews. No free-pooping or glass containers allowed.

First 20 miles are smooth easy climbing. Then in 5 miles drop 3300 ft. on rough-as-heck jeep trail. Do not attempt after dark, full moon or no. Protect the big head. Wear a helmet. This is dangeroso even in daylight. Brakes must be perfect. Because it's rated double-secret-R for nudity AND you're the sort who reads this prurient smut, you'll have the time of your life. If not, hold your nose and close your eyes!

**DANGER & WARNING: DO NOT ATTEMPT TO CROSS VERDE RIVER DURING SPRING HIGH WATER RUNOFF UNLESS I AM IN YOUR WILL!**

"May your trails be crooked, winding, lonesome, dangerous
and leading to the most amazing views."
- Ed Abbey

**HOT SPRINGS**

# BILL WILLIAMS MOUNTAIN

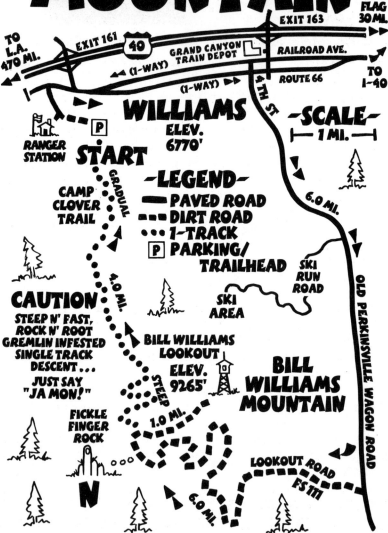

TO FLAG 30 MI.

EXIT 163

EXIT 161

US 40

(1-WAY)

GRAND CANYON TRAIN DEPOT

RAILROAD AVE.

ROUTE 66

TO I-40

TO L.A. 470 MI.

(1-WAY)

4TH ST.

WILLIAMS
ELEV. 6770'

RANGER STATION

P

START

SCALE
— 1 MI. —

6.0 MI.

CAMP CLOVER TRAIL

GRADUAL

-LEGEND-
—— PAVED ROAD
- - - DIRT ROAD
•••• 1-TRACK
P PARKING/ TRAILHEAD

SKI RUN ROAD

4.0 MI.

CAUTION
STEEP N' FAST,
ROCK N' ROOT
GREMLIN INFESTED
SINGLE TRACK
DESCENT...
JUST SAY
"JA MON!"

SKI AREA

BILL WILLIAMS LOOKOUT ELEV. 9265'

BILL WILLIAMS MOUNTAIN

STEEP

FICKLE FINGER ROCK

1.0 MI.

N

6.0 MI.

LOOKOUT ROAD
FS 111

OLD PERKINSVILLE WAGON ROAD

NO COPIES PLEASE!

# WILLIAMS

© RAY
© 1998

# Williams BILL WILLIAMS MTN.
## LOOP RIDE TO SINGLE TRACK DESCENT

**DISTANCE:** 20 MILES
**TIME:** 3 HOURS
**EFFORT:** NOT TOO TOUGH
**SKILL:** INTERMEDIATE
**PUCK-O-METER:** PUCK 8
HIGH SPEED DESCENT WITH HAZARDS
**FIND ROUTE:** EASY
**SEASON:** APR to OCT

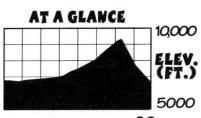

**AT A GLANCE**

10,000

**ELEV. (FT.)**

5000

O  **LOOP MILES**  20

**DESCRIPTION:** Log hops, trail gremlins, boulders, steep switchbacks and even an early morning mound of steaming black bear poop blocked my single track descent!

This is a two water bottle, small chainwheel, bring-a-snack, lose-the-dog type jaunt to the top of Bill Williams Mountain via The Old Perkinsville Wagon Road, Bill Williams Lookout Road and finishing up with a quickie, tricky descent down the old girls' camp Camp Clover Trail. That latter is now renamed Bill Williams Trail as I reckon not too many old girls could handle the descent, although I thought it was brilliant twisty-turny fast fun!

A blue spruce and aspen forest lines the ascent, giving you plenty of nice stuff to zone out on during the climb. The *plein aire* view from Bill Williams Lookout stretches west to California, east to the San Francisco Peaks, north to The Canyon and south deep into the purple haze. There's even a side trip to Finger Rock, a towering volcanic plug signaling a dubious welcome to travellers from The Golden State on I-40 far below.

The tiny burg of Williams is worth a visit. Picture a town that survives peddling Route 66 memorabilia and The Grand Canyon steam train. It's funky and fun. You can even get a decent cappuccino at *Grand Canyon Coffee & Cafe* on W. Route 66. Route 66?! Williams was the last holdout of *The Mother Road* bypassed by boring, mind numbing, sleep inducing interstate freeway.

**DIRECTIONS:** From Flagstaff drive west on I-40 to the last Williams exit #161. Go over the freeway then RIGHT to the Williams Ranger Station parking lot START.

"Horn broken. Watch for finger (rock)."
-bumper sticker

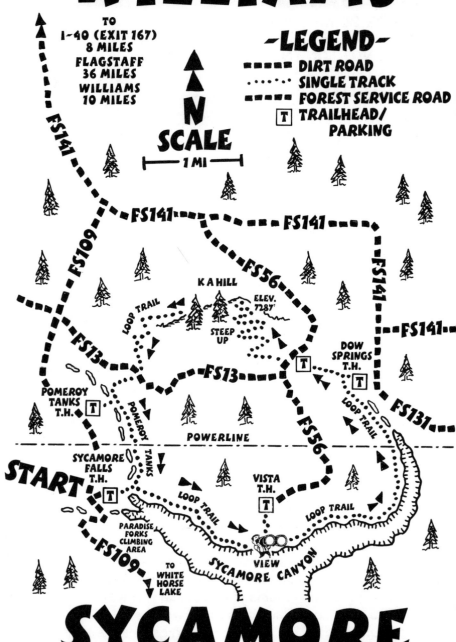

# WILLIAMS

TO
I-40 (EXIT 167)
8 MILES
FLAGSTAFF
36 MILES
WILLIAMS
10 MILES

**N**
**SCALE**
⊢—— 1 MI ——⊣

## -LEGEND-

- ▪▪▪▪ **DIRT ROAD**
- ∙∙∙∙∙∙ **SINGLE TRACK**
- ▪ ▪ ▪ **FOREST SERVICE ROAD**
- T **TRAILHEAD/ PARKING**

FS141

FS109

FS141

FS141

FS56

FS141

FS141

K A HILL

ELEV. 7287'

LOOP TRAIL

STEEP UP

FS13

DOW SPRINGS T.H.

T

FS131

LOOP TRAIL

POMEROY TANKS T.H.

T

FS13

POMEROY TANKS

POWERLINE

FS56

LOOP TRAIL

START

SYCAMORE FALLS T.H.

T

VISTA T.H.

T

LOOP TRAIL

LOOP TRAIL

PARADISE FORKS CLIMBING AREA

VIEW

FS109

TO WHITE HORSE LAKE

SYCAMORE CANYON

# SYCAMORE RIM LOOP

RAY
© 1999

# Williams SYCAMORE RIM LOOPS
## SINGLE TRACK FREERIDE TO VIEWS

**DISTANCE:** 11 MILES
**TIME:** 2 TO 4 HOURS
**EFFORT:** NOT FOR WIMPS
**SKILL:** FAIRLY MODERATE
**PUCK-O-METER:** PUCK 4
**FIND ROUTE:** SIGNED
**SEASON:** SATAN'S OWN MUD WHEN WET!

AT A GLANCE

7400

ELEV. (FT.)

6400

O  LOOP MILES  11

**DESCRIPTION:** Sycamore Rim Trail runs you along the very edge of the top of Sycamore Canyon. There is a short loop, a longer loop, great swimming holes, sheer cliffs, a short, stout climb and fast descent, smooth 1-track runs, rocky sections and great views. In short, everything. The trail is partly smooth, but it can be rough and tough or muddy in bursts, especially in the section between Pomeroy Tanks and Sycamore Falls. Best to do this bone banger, not-for-wimps loop during dry months after winter has dried and summer monsoon is absent.

Route finding may be a bit tricky due to a surplus of fancy but confusing signs. However, the cairns are great. I found it best to ignore anything relating to the "Overland Trail", a horse route, ghost trail that bisects the Rim Trail Loop adding nothing but confusion. Just pay attention to cairns, Rim Trail signs and the power line/bail trail that neatly bisects the area.

Start at Sycamore Falls. That way you can do the rim view trail first, the big hill in the middle and the cool swimming holes at the end. Also, you can bail on the final tough section between Pomeroy Tanks and Sycamore Falls via smooth dirt road if you've had enough.

**DIRECTIONS:** From Flagstaff go west on I-40 for 28 miles toward Williams. Get off at Exit #167 (Garland Prairie Road) Next, ignore all confusing words and arrows on the forest circus signs that follow. PAY ATTENTION TO THE NUMBERS. Go south on FS 141 for 8 miles to FS 109. Turn RIGHT on Fs 109 and go 3.4 miles to the Sycamore Falls Trailhead on your left. Start there.

*"Be good and you will be lonesome."*
*Mark Twain*

**WILLIAMS**

# G-NARLY G-LOSSARY
## OF ARCANE TRAIL JARGON
### (THE BURLACIOUS WORDAGE!)

**AFEARD:** Nothing to fear but feard itself.
**AIR:** To launch or fly. Sky it. Fly it. Hairy air.
**AMPED:** Psyched, wired, stoked or even go ballistic.
**ANNO:** Anodized parts. Purple is sooo over. Rasta anno *still* rocks.
**AUGER:** Wreck. Crater. Stack. Do a digger.
**BACON:** Scabby trail jerky. Road rash.
**BAIL:** Quit. Exit. Weenie out. Go home.
**BAD DOG:** Pit bull on crack. Hard ride.
**BAKED:** Used up. Burnt, busted or bent.
**BARNEY RIDE:** Rubble and rocky debris.
**BEAVER BREATHER:** Seat with a hole.
**BELLY TART:** Sour bark up after big eat.
**BETTY:** Nice. Plush. Fine. Smooth. Easy. A betty ride.
**BIFF:** Bite. Stack. Crash. Dig. Wipe. Wreck. See auger.
**BOING:** Bounce. Full boing. Suspension.
**BOMBER:** Stout. Way burly. Tough.
**BONK:** Your body is baked. Outa gas.
**BUFF:** Ripped musculature. Perfecto bike or trail.
**BUNNY HOP:** Hop like bunny over stuff.
**BURR:** Burly. Honkin'. Mondo gnurly. Way burr, dude.
**BUTT FUR:** That what gets ruffed on a butt ruff.
**BUTT RUFF:** Not rough enough to stand, but too rough to ride seated.
**BUZZ:** The buzz. Word around the campfire. Buzzed. Wired. Excited.
**CAGER:** Motorist. Person trapped in a car.
**CARVE:** Rip, rail, cut or tear a turn.
**CHOP:** The chop. Washboards. Rough stuff.
**CHUB:** Chubby. Excited. Engorged elation. To get one.
**CLEAN:** Clear all obstacles. Nail it.
**CLOTHESLINE:** Dismounted by rope or wire. Decapitation points.
**CLYDESDALE:** Big boy mountain biker.
**COMMANDO:** To go commando. Go off trail . Go without undies. Ouch.
**COSMIC:** The yin and yang. Balance in all things.
**COSMIC RAY:** Stream of atomic nuclei from space.
**CRATER:** Auger. Wreck. Especially to dig using head for shovel.
**CURB GRIND:** Wreck on rocks. To "roach it" on a curb grind.
**CUSTOM:** Innovative bike repair. Custom retro.
**DAB:** To touch down or not clean an obstacle.
**DIAL:** Fine tune. Precision perfect dynamo hummmm.
**DIPPED:** Stoked. Happy. Dipped in doo.
**DIRT SQUIRT:** Mutant offspring. Grommet. Bike child.
**DOUBLE TRACK:** 2-track. Jeep road.
**EFFLUVIA:** Bugs, dirt, snot, sputum and spit. The crap on your glasses.
**EPIC:** Siege shred. Hairball bloodbath. Hard ride.
**E-TICKET:** Epic scary, hairy, fun ride. Total hairball.
**FASHION FELONY:** Neon. Skunkbutt togs.
**FAT:** Large, big, portly, rotund, thick, corpulent, chubby.
**FATTY:** Twisted up fat one.
**FUN:** Very elastic term to describe almost anything. Often hateful.
**GAK:** Cough, hack or hork. Phlegm points.
**GHOST RIDE:** You bail, bike wrecks alone.
**GIBLETS:** After market add on bike parts. Bolt-ons.
**GRANNY:** Small gear reduction. Nice old lady.
**GRAVITY SCHOOL:** Mè magna cum laude.
**HAIRBALL:** So scary as to require the amount of hair to weave a wool rug.
**HAMMER:** To pound. To pedal or ride hard and fast. A hammerfest.
**HARSH:** Rough. As in, "Dude, don't harsh my shred."

BACON

**HEADBANGER:** Nutcase. Haircut with attitude.
**H.O.H.:** Hateful old hiker.
**HOOKY:** Grippy trail that hooks up like velcro.
**HORK:** Toss. Throw. Huck your HO-HOs up or down.
**J.R.A.:** I wuz just riding along when . . . Warranty fraud.
**LAWYER TABS:** Hateful tabs on fork tips.
**MACHIN':** 740 m.p.h. = mach 1. Going very fast.
**MONGO:** Giganto humongo as in way killer mongo.
**MOTO:** Worthy shreddage. Nice bike or trail.
**MULCH IT:** To turf it in the sticks and weeds.
**MUTANT:** Tweaked out mountain bike maniac.
**NIG-NOG:** Wig-wag corndog. A ding-dong.
**NO WAY:** Hans Ray. Yes way.
**OBSERVED TRIALS:** Risk the nuts doing stupid stuff.
**OFF BEAT:** Off kilter. Irregular. Half bubble off level.
**OILED:** Lubricated. Intoxicated.
**O.T.B.:** Over the bars.
**P.L.F.:** Parachute landing fall. Leg, hip, side roll. Good luck.
**POGO GEEK:** Trials maneuverist.
**POSER:** Lycra ding-dong. A Fred. Possibly a full on MTV nig nog.
**POUND:** Hammer with gusto as in pound java or pound the dog.
**PSYCHO:** Disturbing behavior. Hateful headbanger.
**PUCK-O-METER:** Fear factor. Pucker factor.
**RAD:** Wicked cool. The bomb. The freak.
**RAGER:** A radical ride or rider.
**RETRO-GROUCH:** Technophobic coot.
**RHOID BUFF:** Butt contacts rolling rear tire. OW!
**RIGGED-TO-FLIP:** Secured by all manner of wire and tape.
**ROACH:** Roach it. Wreck. Icky bug.
**ROCK GARDEN:** Eyeball- rattling, tooth-banging hell.
**ROOKIE MARK:** Chain grease mark on leg. Points for wrong leg.
**RUBBLING:** Wreck in rubble. To go jeeping.
**SALAD BAR:** Turf it in the shrubbery. The shmorgy of shred.
**SHOTGUN:** Blow-&-go on the fly nose blow.
**SHRED:** A fine ride or pleasant experience.
**SHUCKS:** Expletive denoting bitter disappointment.
**SHWAG:** Swag. Loot. Free bike stuff. Gimme some!
**SHWANK:** Swank. As in shwanky shwag.
**SKANKY:** Groaty, gooey, messy and gross. As a bike chain.
**SKINNY:** Tires ridden by nerds, geeks, dweebs and feebs.
**SLICK ROCK:** Humongo smooth stones to ride.
**SNORKLED:** Too busy at work. No time to ride.
**SOCK WASH:** Laundry. Trail through creek or wet grass.
**SPHINCTER PHACTOR:** Puck-o-meter scale in degrees of repose (1 to 10).
**SPOOGE:** Skanky, gooey, groaty, gross grime and guck. Oh wretch.
**STINK EYE:** Getting "THE LOOK" from a hiker. See H.O.H.
**STYLIN':** Styling. On deck. Possible poser factor.
**SUCK AND SLAP:** The misbehaving evil chain twins.
**TACO:** Bent wheel resembling same or potato chip.
**TECH WEENIE:** Poser nig-nog with the latest cool stuff.
**THRASH:** To trash, bash or smash. Mutated video music.
**TOSS:** Throw, spew, hurl and hork. Frequently enchilada style.
**TRIALS:** Tribulations. Obstacle course. Skill test.
**TUNED:** Dialed, tooned, tweaked, psyched, buzzed and hot wired.
**URGE:** Power, drive, energy, desire and surge.
**VELCRO:** Hooky or grippy trail surface.
**VERT:** Big vertical steepness. To fly or go vertical.
**WEENIE:** Whimpering, whining weakling.
**WEENIE WALK:** Sketchy or steep as to cause weenies to walk.
**WORKABLE:** Do-able section along the road to hell.
**YARD SALE:** Big wreck scatters your stuff here to there.

CRATER

MUTANT

ROOKIE MARK

SPHINCTER PHACTOR

CURB GRIND

WEENIE WALK

# BACKTALK!

*Greetings earthling!* I am Cosmic Ray. Half man, half wit. Been burning the candle at both ends, holding the lighter in my teeth and teaching the daughter to ride her very own first real mountain bike. Dangerous? Not to worry. The burly *NEW MIGHTY MILLENNIUM* (14th) *EDITION* is here. Less reading, more riding and 100% guaranteed *NOT* to be the normal homogenized dookie dished up by some dufus corndog armchair mountain biker who's never gone over the bars, wrecked big time, gotten lost or scared. Heck, *that's every ride!*

My semi-accurate treasure maps still look a bit like the primitive doggerel of a demented adolescent. I am a bike mechanic by trade. Be thankful. They used to look the scribble of some crazed out mutant bike rat on glue. My maps are rough like mountain biking, not an exact science. It's hard dirty fun that frequently hurts. Real sport for real people.

Pals Micah, Eric, Jane, Tom and myself are to blame for the art. Greg, Lowell and Wally print the thing. Dave sells it and keeps me reeled in. Extra special thanks to all my ultra gnarly buds who tell me jokes, listen to mine, turn me on to favorite rides and put me up on their couches all over Arizona while I test 'em out. The rides, silly, not the couches! Wait, there's more.

The hardcores need credit . . . them what puts up with my nut case self every day . . . my way groovy friends, my mom and pop who bought all those first bikes, Marcia with whom I share every secret and especially daughter and Cosmic Dirt Squirt Elena Marie. *Wild Thing, you make my heart sing!*

Cosmic Ray and Fat Tire Friend, October 21, 1954

COSMIC RAY 3960 N ZURICH ST. FLAGSTAFF, AZ 86004
e-mail: cosray@aol.com    fax: (520) 526-8243

# ARIZONA MOUNTAIN BIKE YELLOW PAGES

Please FAX additions, deletions, corrections or whatever to
(520) 526-8243 or e-mail to COSRAY@AOL.COM

## AHWATUKEE

CYCLE SPECTRUM, 4405 E. Ray Rd.................................................................................480 833-7195
SMC / FUN SPORTS, 3636 E. Ray Rd...............................................................................480 706-0858

## APACHE JUNCTION

JUNCTION BICYCLES, 10839 E. Apache Trail ...................................................... 480 380-0811

## BULLHEAD CITY

TRI STATE BIKES, 1868 HWY 95 .......................................................................... 520 758-7400
CYCLE THERAPY, 1710 Lakeside Drive ............................................................... 520-763-3553

## CASA GRANDE

ROUND TRIP BIKE SHOP, 1144 E. Florence Blvd..............................................520 836-0799

## CAVE CREEK

CAVE CREEK BICYCLES, 6249 E. Cave Creek Rd. .............................................. 480 488-5261

## **SPOKESMAN BICYCLES**, 29605 N. Cave Creek Rd. ............. **480 342-9200**

## CHANDLER

## **ARIZONA BIKE SOURCE,** 2051 N. Arizona Ave. ......................... **480 786-3660**

## **SUPERGO**, 5955 W. Ray Rd. ...................................................... **480 705-9001**

## COTTONWOOD

MINGUS MOUNTAIN BICYCLES, 418 N. 15th St. (15th & Main)....................................520 634-7113

## FLAGSTAFF

## **ABSOLUTE BIKES**, 18 N. San Francisco St. ...................... **520 779-5969**

BICI MUNDO de Elson, 222 E. Brannon Av. ............................................................520 779-3121
BRYCE'S BIKE LOFT, 1608 N. East St. .....................................................................520 773-9881

## **COSMIC CYCLES**, 901 N. Beaver St............................................ **520 779-1092**

(CONTINUED)

### FLAGSTAFF (CONTINUED)

**FLAGSTAFF BIKE & FITNESS,** 2404 E. Route 66 ............... 520  526-2780
**SWITCHBACK SHUTTLE FLAGSTAFF TO SEDONA** ........ 520 774-2200
**LOOSE SPOKE,** 1529 S. Milton Rd. ........................ 520  774-7428
**MOUNTAIN SPORTS,** 1800 S. Milton ...................... 520  779-5156
**SINAGUA CYCLES,** 113 S. San Francisco St. .......................... 520  779-9969
SINGLE TRACK BIKES, 575 Riordan Rd. ................................................................ 520 773-1862

### FOUNTAIN HILLS

**CG BIKES , 16605 E. Palisades Blvd. #120** ................... 480-836-8827

### GILBERT

**BIKE CHALET,** 1130 N. Gilbert Rd. ............................... 480  545-5075

### GLENDALE

ARROWHEAD CYCLERY, 4330 W. Union Hills Dr. ................................................. 623 581-2156
BIKESPORT, 12035 N. 59th Ave. .................................................................. 623 979-3474
CROSSROADS, 20211 N. 67th Ave. ............................................................... 623 561-1007
GOLDEN SPOKE CYCLERY, 4703 W. Olive .................................................... 623 931-8910
GORDY'S BICYCLES, 4920 W. Thunderbird ................................................ 602 843-6490
ROAD RUNNER, 5930 W. Greenway #24 ...................................................... 602 547-2350
**SWISS AMERICAN BIKE CTR. , 16835 N. Park Place** ........ 602  938-4330

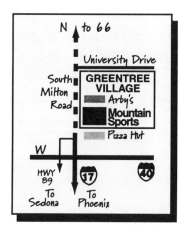

## Sinaqua Cycles

**EST. 1999**

**Saving the World One Bike At A Time**

# Service • Sales • Rentals

Daily Group Rides • 30 Years Combined Mt. Bike Experience
New • Used • Vintage • Consignment • 1 Speeds
The Southwest's Leading Single Speed Dealer

**779-9969 • Open 7 days in Spring & Summer • Call for Hours**
**113 S. San Francisco St. • Flagstaff, AZ 86001**

### GOOD YEAR
EVERGREEN BIKE, 880 E. Van Buren ............................................................623 932-0060
### GREEN VALLEY
BJ'S BIKE SHOP, 271 W. Calle de las Tiendas ...............................................520 625-0206
### HAVASU CITY
CYCLE THERAPY, 2144 N. McCulloch Blvd. ...................................................520-855-3553
MBK, 76 N. Lake Havasu Ave. ........................................................................520 453-7474
### KINGMAN
BICYCLE WORLD, 1825 Northern Ave. ...........................................................520-757-5730
CACTUS CYCLERY, 4055 Stockton Hill Rd. ....................................................520 757-7335

### MESA
**A-1 BIKE CENTER, 3725 E. Southern #6** ..................... **480 641-0819**
**ADVENTURE BICYCLE CO.,** 1110 W. Southern ..................... **480 649-3394**
BICYCLE WORLD, 6132 E. Main St. ................................................................480 985-4772
**BIKE CHALET,** 5761 E. Brown Rd. ...................................... **480 807-2944**
CYCLE SPECTRUM, 1720 W. Southern .............................................................480 833-7195
CYCLE SPECTRUM, 1545 S. Power Rd. ............................................................480 981-8901
EAST VALLEY, 7919 E. Apache Trail ...............................................................480 986-9188
**PAT'S SCHWINN CYCLERY,** 929 E. Main St. ..................... **480 964-3330**
**PAT'S SCHWINN CYCLERY,** 1042 N. Higley Road ............... **480 981-0468**
### PAYSON
**MANZANITA CYCLERY,** 321 E. Hwy 260 .......................... **520 474-0744**

# TEMPE BICYCLE

www.tempebicycle.com

## (480) 966-6896

## 330 W. UNIVERSITY
## (4 BLOCKS WEST OF MILL)

### PEORIA

**PEORIA DOUBLE WHEEL**, 10545 N. 83rd Ave. ..................... **623  486-8565**

**SOUTHWEST BICYCLES**, 8155 W. Bell Rd. .......................... **623  412-3150**

### PHOENIX

**BICYCLE SHOWCASE**, 3102 E. Cactus.................................. **602  971-0730**

**BICYCLE WAREHOUSE**, 4036 N. 19th Ave. ........................ **602  265-0660**

BIKE AGE, 318 N. 48th St. ...................................................... 602 275-8113

**BIKE BARN**, 4112 N. 36th St. .............................................. **602  956-3870**

**BIKE DEN, LTD.**, 4312 W. Cactus ...................................... **602  938-1289**

**DOUBLE WHEEL STORES**, 6727 W. Indian School Rd........ **623  846-1997**

**DOUBLE WHEEL STORES METRO**, 3424 W. Peoria.......... **602  942-2453**

EXCELLENT BIKES, 2814 W. Bell Rd. ........................................602 548-0567

**LANDIS CYCLERY**, 712 W. Indian School Rd. ...................... **602  264-5681**

PARADISE VALLEY BICYCLES, 4727 E. Bell Rd...............................602 788-0808

PHOENIX BICYCLES, 3033 N. 24th St. ........................................602 954-0650

RECUMBENT CENTRAL, 6522 N. 16th St..................................602 230-2393

REI, 12634 N. Paradise Village Pkwy W. .....................................602 996-5400

CONTINUED

## PHOENIX (CONTINUED)

SLIPPERY PIG BIKE SHOP, 5036 N. Central Ave. ........................... 602 263-5143

**SOUTHWEST BICYCLES,** 401 E. Bell Rd............................... **602 375-1515**

**SUN CYCLERY,** 5833 N. 7TH St.................................... **602 279-1905**

TRY ME BICYCLES, 1514 W. Hatcher .................................... 602 943-1785

**VALLEY CYCLERY,** 751 E. Bell Rd. ................................ **602 942-3733**

TATUM CYCLERY, 4611 E. Cactus ...................................... 602 494-2999

### PRESCOTT

**BIKESMITH CYCLE,** 723 N. Montezuma St. ......................... **520 445-0280**

**HIGH GEAR,** 237 N. Mount Vernon Ave............................ **520 445-8417**

IRONCLAD BICYCLES, 710 White Spar Rd. ................................ 520 776-1755

**MOUNTAIN SPORTS,** 142 N. Cortez St. ........................... **520 445-8310**

DIRT WORKS BIKES, 8194-B Ashley Dr., (PRESCOTT VALLEY) ................... 520 775-4860

### SAFFORD

CYCLE PATH, 726 S. 6th Ave............................................... 520 428-4666

# SWITCHBACK SHUTTLE

SNOWBOWL

WILLIAMS — **FLAGSTAFF**

SEDONA

**(520) 774-2200**
**WWW.SWITCHBACKSHUTTLE.COM**

PHOENIX

## SCOTTSDALE

| | | |
|---|---|---|
| **AIRPARK BICYCLES**, 8666 E. Shea | 480 | 480-6633 |
| BICYCLE RANCH, 15454 N. Frank Lloyd Wright | | 480 614-8300 |
| **BICYCLE SHOWCASE**, 7229 E. Shea | 480 | 998-2776 |
| BIKE EMPORIUM, 8433 E. McDonald Dr, | | 480 991-5430 |
| **BIKE WAREHOUSE**, 4408 N. Miller Rd | 480 | 949-7106 |
| BOB'S BIKE SHOP, 1608 N. Miller Rd. | | 480 946-9461 |
| JAANUS BICYCLES, 14950 N. 83rd Place | | 480 922-0111 |
| **LANDIS CYCLERY**, 10417 N. Scottsdale Rd. | 480 | 948-9280 |
| PINNACLE PEAK CYCLERY, 23269 N. Pima #H123 | | 480 473-4601 |
| **RAGE BICYCLES**, 2724 N. Scottsdale Rd. | 480 | 968-8116 |
| **VALLEY CYCLERY**, 15576 N. Pima Rd. | 480 | 483-8020 |
| WHEELS & GEAR, 7607 E. McDowell | | 480 945-2881 |

## SEDONA

| | | |
|---|---|---|
| **MOUNTAIN BIKE HEAVEN**, 1695 Hwy 89A | 520 | 282-1312 |
| **SEDONA BIKE & BEAN**, 6020 HWY 179, V.O.C. | 520 | 284-0210 |
| **SWITCHBACK SHUTTLE SEDONA TO FLAGSTAFF** | 520 | 774-2200 |
| **SEDONA SPORTS**, 251 HWY 179, #1A | 520 | 282-1317 |

## We Roast
## We Bake     We Brew
## We Ride!

**Three Locations:**

1800 N. Fort Valley Road (**Hwy. 180** to Snowbowl)
107 N. San Francisco (**Downtown** N. of tracks)

**And just in case...**

FMC **Hospital** (Main Lobby off Beaver St.)

### SHOW LOW
CYCLE MANIA, 4350 S. White Mtn. Rd. ................................................520 537-8812

### SIERRA VISTA
M&M CYCLING, 1301 E. Fry Blvd. ....................................................520 458-1316
**SUN & SPOKES**, 164 Fry Blvd. ..................................................**520 458-0685**

### TEMPE
BICYCLE STORE, 19 E. 9th St. ........................................................480 966-7090
BICYCLE STORE, 1035 E. Lemon ....................................................480 966-6070
**BICYCLE WHEELERS**, 2010 S. Rural Rd. ......................................**480 968-8011**
CYCLE SPECTRUM, 1805 E. Elliott ..................................................480 491-5544
**DOMENIC'S CYCLING**, 1004 S. Mill Ave. ......................................**480 967-779**

CONTINUED

# ARIZONA MOUNTAIN BIKE YELLOW PAGES

## TEMPE (CONTINUED)

EHRHARDT'S SCHWINN, 111 E. University Dr. ................................480 967-2137

**LANDIS CYCLERY,** 2180 E. Southern ...................................... **480 839-9383**

**LANDIS CYCLERY,** 1006 E. Warner.......................................... **480 730-1081**

REI, 1405 W. Southern.................................................................480 967-5494

**TEMPE BICYCLE,** 330 W. University Dr................................... **480 966-6896**

## TUCSON

AJO BIKES, 3816 S. 12th Ave.....................................................520 294-1434

ARIZONA CYCLE & SPORT, 2716 S. Kolb ....................................520 750-1454

ARIZONA BIKE EXPERTS, 2520 E. 6th St. ...................................520 881-2279

BARGAIN BASEMENT BIKES, 428 N. Fremont..............................520 624-9673

BICYCLE REVOLUTION, 1058 N. Campbell ..................................520-319-9294

CONTINUED

## TUCSON (CONTINUED)

|  |  |
|---|---|
| BICYCLES WEST, 3801 No. Oracle Rd. | 520 887-7770 |
| BROADWAY BICYCLES, 140 S. Sarnoff | 520 296-7819 |
| BROADWAY SCHWINN, 7004 E. Broadway | 520 296-4715 |
| CATALINA BICYCLE SHOP, 2310 N. Campbell | 520 326-7377 |
| CYCLE SPECTRUM, 7177 E. Broadway | 520 790-9394 |
| FAIR WHEEL BIKES, 1110 E. 6thSt. | 520 884-9018 |
| FULL CYCLE, 3302 E. Speedway | 520 327-3232 |
| LONE CACTUS CYCLES, 8779 E. Broadway | 520 885-3092 |
| ORDINARY BIKE SHOP, 741 E. 4th Ave. | 520 622-6488 |
| PIMA STREET BICYCLES,5247 E. Pima St. | 520 326-4044 |
| R & R ORACLE ROAD BICYCLES, 7937 N. Oracle | 520 575-5594 |
| R & R BICYCLE, 3757 W. Ina Rd. | 520 579-7829 |
| SABINO CYCLES, 7131 E. Tanque Verde | 520 885-3666 |
| SPEEDWAY BICYCLES,3013 E. Speedway Blvd. | 520 795-3339 |
| TUCSON BICYCLES, 4743 E. Sunrise Dr. | 520 577-7374 |

### YUMA

|  |  |
|---|---|
| MR. B'S, 1870 S. 4th Ave. | 520 782-0028 |
| MR B'S, 1701 S. Avenue B., #115 | 520 343-7802 |
| MR B'S, 11242 Foothills Blvd. | 520 342-2957 |

Work like you don't need the money.
Love like you've never been hurt.
Dance (& ride) like nobody's watching.
- Cosmic Proverb